20/9

D0867047

PHILOSOPHY / *An Introduction*

J. M. Bocheński / PHILOSOPHY

AN INTRODUCTION

D. REIDEL PUBLISHING COMPANY

DORDRECHT/HOLLAND

WEGE ZUM PHILOSOPHISCHEN DENKEN
First published by Verlag Herder KG
Freiburg im Breisgau, Germany
Translated by William M. Newell

Printed in The Netherlands by D. Reidel, Dordrecht

Table of Contents

page   6   TRANSLATOR'S NOTE

         7   FOREWORD

         9   LAW

     20   PHILOSOPHY

     31   KNOWLEDGE

     42   TRUTH

     53   THINKING

     63   VALUES

     73   MAN

     83   BEING

     93   SOCIETY

    102   THE ABSOLUTE

TRANSLATOR'S NOTE / In this, as in all translations of philosophical works, there are certain words or phrases which will most likely strike the reader, at first glance, as awkward or unorthodox. Such difficulties, although undesirable, cannot be avoided. A German philosophical text of this nature contains some substantives which have no standard or philosophical equivalent in English. The word *sein*, for example, when expanded into *Seiende* assumes a meaning which is not quite captured by the English 'being'. In an effort to remain true to the original text but yet avoid ambiguities, I have used some expressions which are to be understood only in a very narrow and defined way. At times, this has resulted in a certain unevenness but, in a work of this type, stylistic smoothness must be sacrificed for clarity and precision.

I am greatly indebted to Ernest Hankamer of Munich, Germany, for his helpful suggestions in clarifying many points of the German text, and for his aid in examining the entire translation. His assistance has been invaluable. The translator is responsible, of course, for any remaining inaccuracies or inconsistencies.

Munich, June 1962

Foreword

These ten lectures were held on the 'Special Program' of the Bavarian Radio during May, June and July of 1958. For publication, I have changed the text only in small stylistic details; otherwise it remains for the reader as it was given on the radio.

This may also explain the special character of this small volume. Its content is of a very popular nature. Naturally, I can make no claim to completeness, either in the listing of philosophical directions or in the presentation of problems. My goal was rather to explain to those listeners unoriented in philosophy, by means of some problems, what philosophy is and how it approaches its objects. Therefore, it cannot be objected — although I regret it myself — that, for example, the 'existentialist' concept of man, the Hegelian objective mind and similar things haven't even been mentioned. A choice had to be made, and the short time of twenty seven minutes sometimes forced me to delete some things already written.

These discussions could have been carried out actually in two ways. One would be the 'objective', non-partisan presentation of some views without the author's revealing his own point of view. The other consists in maintaining a certain standpoint from the very outset, and then discussing the problems as well as the solutions in relation to it. I consciously chose the second method because the first seemed simply impossible to me. For, and this is my opinion, there isn't and can't be an 'objective' presentation, in the above mentioned sense, of the basic

7

philosophical problems. The point of view which is here expressed is naturally that of the author. Thus, this series of discussions became something completely different from what I had originally intended, that is, a brief, but perhaps clear, presentation of a philosophy, the philosophy which I hold to be true.

This publication appears in the hope that some of my readers would like to have the text of the lectures, and further that it might facilitate, for others, the approach to philosophical thinking.

Law

TODAY I WOULD like to reflect upon law with you. I do not mean those laws which are determined by parliament and applied by the courts, but rather law in the scientific sense of the word – physical, chemical and biological laws, especially laws of the pure, abstract sciences, as in the various branches of mathematics.

Everyone knows that there are such laws. It also should be clear that they are of enormous importance for all of human life. For law is that which has been established by science, and from which our technology has been formed. Law is that which is clear and certain, the ultimate basis of every rational action. Were we to have no natural laws, no mathematical laws, then we would be mere barbarians, helpless beings exposed to the sway of natural forces. It is hardly an exaggeration when I say that we know few things which are so vitally important for us as laws; – among others, or perhaps above all, the mathematical, pure laws.

Now, there are men who are prepared to make use of an instrument without knowing the slightest thing about its construction. I know radio reporters who don't even know whether their microphone is a ribbon or a condenser apparatus, and drivers who only know where the starter is in their cars. In fact, it seems to me that the number of such automatic men who use everything and understand nothing is becoming larger and larger. It is a frightful fact that only a few of most radio listeners are interested in the structure of this wonder of technology, the receiver.

But even if it were so that most of us have lost all interest in technical equipment, still it can be hoped that this is not the case with the law. For the law is not only an instrument. It affects our lives deeply, it is the condition of our culture; it is, as we said, the element of clarity and rationality in our view of the world.

And for this reason it seems to me that for once we should ask the question: What is a law?

Merely asking this question and reflecting on it a bit suffices to make us realize that a law is something very remarkable and singular. This can be best shown perhaps in the following manner.

The world around us consists of many and varied things, but all of these things – Beings, as the philosophers say – have certain common characteristics. By thing or being I mean here everything that is to be encountered in the world – men, animals, mountains, stones and so forth. The common characteristics of these things are, among others, the following:

First, all of these things are in some *place* – for example, I am in Fribourg and am sitting at my desk. Then they exist during a particular *time* – for me, it is today, Monday, twelve o'clock. Third, we know of no thing which did not *come to be* at some point in time, and, as far as we know, all things are transitory. A time comes when they disappear. Fourth, they are all subject to change; man may now be healthy, another time sick – a tree is once small, then it grows larger, and so forth. Fifth, each of these things is *singular*, individual. I am I and no other, this mountain is precisely this mountain and no other mountain. Everything that is in this world is individual, singular.

Finally, and this is very important, every known thing in the world *could be otherwise* or not at all. To be sure, some men believe that they are necessary, but this is an error. They could also not exist, and probably without too great a loss for the whole.

These are, therefore, the characteristics of everything in the world. Everything is in a certain place, at a certain time, everything comes to be, passes away, changes, is individual and not necessary. Such is the world; or at least so it seems to be.

But now, into this cozy spatial, temporal, and transient world consisting of many individual things comes the law.

But the law has *none* of the above-mentioned characteristics of things – *not one*.

For, first of all, it would be absolutely senseless to say that a mathematical law exists at any given place; if it exists, then it exists everywhere equally. Of course, I make an image of this law in my head, but that is only an image. The law is not identical with this image, but rather external. It is beyond all space.

Second, it is beyond time. It is meaningless to say that a law came to be yesterday, or that it has expired. Indeed it was recognized at a certain point in time, perhaps at another point in time it will be found to be false, that it was no law; but the law itself is timeless.

Third, it is and can be subject to no change. That two and two are four will remain for eternity without change – it would be nonsense to think of changing it.

Finally – and this is perhaps the most remarkable – the law is not individual, it is not singular, it is general. It is to be found here and there, and again somewhere else, *ad infinitum*. For example, we find that two and two are four not only on the earth but also on the moon, and in all of these innumerable cases we have found the same – I emphasize – *the exact same law*.

But this is connected with the most important thing of all. Law is *necessary*, that is, it cannot be other than as it presents itself. Even in the case of the so-called laws of probability which purport that something will happen with this or that probability – but *that* it will happen with precisely *this* and no other probability is necessary. This fact is unique and is to be found nowhere else in the world except in law; for, as we said, every thing in the world is only factual, it could be otherwise. So much for the facts, at least as they seem to be. For *there are* laws, and it appears that they are precisely what we have seen them to be.

But, as we have emphasized, this fact is quite remarkable. The world, our world which we deal with daily, looks completely different from these laws. It is variegated and contains different species of objects; however, everything which it contains has the familiar character of the spatial, temporal, transitory, individual and non-necessary. In this world, how do laws fit in which are non-spatial, timeless, general, eternal, and necessary. Don't they seem to be ghost-like? Wouldn't it be much simpler if they could be explained away somehow, removed from the world so that, in the final analysis, it could be shown that they are basically no different from the usual things of the world? This is the first thought which occurs the moment it becomes clear that there are such things as laws. And from this originates the philosophical problem.

Why do we have a philosophical problem here? The answer is that all other sciences presuppose the fact that there should be laws. They advance laws, investigate them, search for them, but *what* a law is, is of no interest to them. And still the question seems not only meaningful but also of importance. For with the assumption of the law something like another world creeps into our world. But this other world is a bit unpleasant, somewhat ghostlike. Wouldn't it be nice if one could get rid of these laws by a suitable explanation?

In fact, such explanations are not lacking. For example, one can advance the opinion that the laws are products of thought. That would mean that the world would be thoroughly composed of things, that absolutely no laws could be found in it; they would be only fictions of our thinking. In this case, a law would exist only in the mind of the scientist – the mathematician or the physicist, for example. It would be a part of his consciousness.

This solution has actually been recommended often, among others by the great Scottish philosopher, David Hume. He believed that natural laws have their necessity from the fact that one becomes accustomed to them. Thus, for example, when one has seen very often that water boils when heated, one becomes accustomed to this being so. And this habit becomes second nature – man then cannot think other than as he is accustomed. In a similar manner, Hume and his disciples explain other supposed hall-marks of law. At the end of their analysis none of these hall-marks remain; the law reveals itself as something which fits very well into our good old spatial, temporal, transitory, and individual world.

So much for our first possible interpretation. Let us attempt to reflect a bit on it. It must be admitted that it is somehow human; it permits us to explain away the laws with their unpleasant, ghost-like characteristics. And its foundation seems to be truly rational; for it is a fact that we easily get used to various things and then act as though we were under a compulsion. One need think only of the compulsion which the smoker has in smoking cigarettes.

And yet we have many weighty misgivings about this solution.

First, anyone can see that at least *one* fact is *not* explained by this solution. I mean the fact that, in the world, laws are really valid. Let us take the following example: When an engineer plans a bridge, he relies on a great number of physical laws. Now, if one would assume, as Hume does, that all of these laws are only habits of mankind, or more precisely of this engineer, then one must ask how it is possible that a bridge which is correctly planned according to the proper laws will stand solid, whereas one whose planning the engineer has made mistakes will fall apart. How can human habits be decisive for such masses of concrete and iron? It seems as if the laws are only secondarily in the mind of the engineer. Primarily they are valid *for the world*, for iron and concrete, totally independent of whether anyone knows something about them or not. Why should they have this validity if they were only structures of thought?

This objection can be avoided by saying that the world itself is a product of our thought, that we superimpose our own laws upon it. But that is a solution which the proponents of Hume's doctrine – the positivists – along with most of mankind, found to be monstrous. We shall have more to say about this possibility when we come to the theory of knowledge. But for the present we may assume that only a few men would accept it, and therefore we don't need to take it into consideration.

That is the first objection. But there is a second. Even when one transplants laws into thought, this by no means eliminates them. They exist no longer in the outer world, but continue to have validity in our soul. However, the human soul, human thinking, and in general everything that is human is also a part of the world and has all of the characteristics of the worldly – it is objective.

Here, for the first time, we touch upon that remarkable creature that is we ourselves, man. But we cannot yet begin to think about man. However, one thing should be said, and I want to say it with the most precision I can for a whole series of prejudices stand in the way of a correct understanding of our problem.

What I want to say is this: We find in man much that is unique and which is not to be found in the rest of nature. This singularity, uniqueness, this differing from the rest of nature is generally called the spiritual, or the spirit. Now, the spirit is most certainly an interesting phenomenon for philosophizing. But, as different as the spirit is from everything else in

15

the world, still it remains – and thus everything embodied in it – a part of the world, of nature, at least in the sense that it, like this stone, like this tree before my window, like my typewriter, is temporal, spatial, changeable, not necessary, and individual. A timeless spirit is nonsense. It could be that it will endure forever, but, in so far as we know it, *it endures*, it is a temporal thing. Granted that it can survey far reaches of space, but still all spirits which we know are bound to a body and therefore spatial. Above all, the spirit has nothing necessary in it – it could just as well not exist – and to speak of a general spirit is senseless. Every spirit is always the spirit of a *particular* man – it cannot exist in two men, just as a piece of wood cannot exist in two places at the same time.

But if such is the case, then our problem is not solved, merely postponed; if laws are to be found in our spirit it still must be explained *what* exactly they are. For they are certainly *not* a part of our spirit. Perhaps they are *in the spirit*, but only in so far as they are known through it, and therefore they must exist in some manner outside of the spirit.

If, therefore, one transposes the law into the spirit, one clarifies the situation very little and creates at least one great difficulty: it now must be explained why a law belonging solely to the spirit holds such strict sway in the outer world.

For this reason most philosophers have chosen another course. This course consists basically in saying simply that the laws are something independent of us, of our thinking, and of our spirit. It is thereby asserted that they exist, are, or are valid in some way outside of us, that they are only recognized – more or less clearly – by mankind, but not created, just as we cannot create stones, trees, and animals by our mere thinking. That presupposes, the philosophers say, that they form a totally different, second kind of being, of that which is. In this view, therefore, there is in reality – if we want to call it such – something else beside things, realities, namely laws, and their kind and manner of being is called the ideal. It is said that laws belong to ideal being. Expressed differently, there are two basic forms of being – the real and the ideal.

It is not uninteresting to point out that the two above-mentioned interpretations of the law – the positivistic and the, let us say, idealistic (in the broadest sense of the term) – have very little to do with the conflict among the great *Weltanschauungen*. The Christian is by no means bound, by the nature of his belief, to this type of idealism; he believes that there is a God and an immortal soul, but his belief by no means requires him to believe in the ideal. On the other hand, the Communists maintain that everything is material – they mean by this real – but simultaneously assume that there are eternal, necessary laws, not only in thought but also in the world itself. In a certain sense they are, therefore, much more idealistic than the Christians. The conflict is not one of *Weltanschauungen;* it belongs entirely within the realm of philosophy.

Returning to our problem, it must be added that those who recognize the otherness of law – that is, ideal being – are divided, each according to his conception of this ideal, into various schools. This becomes clear the moment one asks what is to be understood by the existence of the ideal, how should one conceive it? There are, generally speaking, three very important answers to this.

The first is: the ideal exists independent of the real, so to speak, in itself; it forms a special world above and beyond the objective world. In this ideal world there is naturally no space nor time, no change and no mere facticity – everything is eternal, pure, unchangeable, and necessary. This conception is often attributed to the creator of our European philosophy, Plato. He was the first to pose the problem of the law and seems to have solved it in the above-mentioned fashion.

The second solution: the ideal does exist, but not separated from the real – it exists only in the real. More precisely, there are, in the world, only certain structures, a certain formation of things which repeats itself, called essences, and they are so formed that the human spirit can detect laws in them. Formulated laws appear only in our thinking, but they have a foundation in the things themselves, and are therefore valid for the world. This is, in a nutshell, the solution of the greatest pupil of Plato, Aristotle, the founder of most sciences.

Finally, there is a third solution which I touched upon in the discussion of positivism. It does not deny that laws are ideal, but believes that the ideal takes place only in thought. That the laws are valid for the world comes from the fact that the structure of things is a projection of the laws of thinking. This is the doctrine of the great German philosopher, Immanuel Kant.

It is no exaggeration to state that almost every important philosopher here in Europe embraced one of these three solutions, or to state that our philosophy has consisted, and consists to a great degree today, of reflections about these three solutions.

Three years ago I took part in a discussion at the well-known American University of Notre Dame, near Chicago, in which more than one hundred and fifty philosophers and logicians participated. All three speakers were mathematical logicians, and everything that was said took on a highly scientific, mathematico-logical form. The discussion lasted, almost without interruption, for two days and three nights. And it dealt with precisely our problem. Professor Alonzo Church, of Princeton, one of the most important mathematical logicians in the world, championed the platonic doctrine essentially just as the old master had once defended it in the agora in Athens. And I must admit that he did so with great success. It is an eternal problem of philosophy: perhaps it is only for us moderns, who know so many laws and for whom they have become so important, that it is so much more pressing than for any other epoch.

Philosophy

PHILOSOPHY is a concern not limited to the specialist; for, as strange as it may seem, there is probably no human being who doesn't philosophize. Or at least every man has moments in his life in which he becomes a philosopher. This is particularly true of our natural scientists, historians, and artists. Sooner or later, all of them concern themselves with philosophy. Of course, I'm not saying that this is of great service to mankind; the books of philosophizing laymen – be they famous physicists, poets or politicians – are usually bad. Too often they present an immature, naive, and mostly false philosophy. But that is secondary here. The important thing is that we all philosophize and, so it seems, must philosophize. Therefore, the question, what philosophy really is, is important for everyone. Unfortunately, this is one of the most difficult philosophical questions. I know of only a few words which have so many meanings as the word philosophy. Just a few weeks ago, I participated in a colloquium of leading European and American thinkers in France. They all spoke about philosophy, but understood entirely different things by this word. We want to examine more closely the various interpretations and then attempt to find a way to comprehension in this veritable swarm of definitions and views.

Now first, there is a view by which philosophy would be a

collective term for everything which cannot, as yet, be treated scientifically. This is the view of Lord Bertrand Russell, for example, and of many of the positivistic philosophers. They point out to us that, for Aristotle, philosophy and science meant the same thing, and that later the individual sciences detached themselves from philosophy; first medicine, then physics, later psychology, finally even formal logic which, as we know, is taught today mostly as a branch of mathematics. Or, to put it another way, there is no philosophy at all in the sense that there is, for example, mathematics, with its special object. There is no such object of philosophy. It is merely a name for certain attempts to clarify or explain various, as yet, immature problems.

This is most certainly an interesting standpoint, and, at first glance, the proposed arguments sound very convincing. But if we look at the matter a little more closely, we begin to have doubts. For first, if these philosophers were right, then we should have less philosophy today than a thousand years ago. But this is certainly not the case. There is not less philosophy today but more than ever. And I don't mean only the number of thinkers – there are about ten thousand today – but also the number of problems discussed. Comparing the philosophy of the ancient Greeks with ours, we can see that we of the twentieth century ask considerably more questions than the Greeks knew.

Second, it is definitely true that various disciplines have detached themselves from philosophy in the course of time. But the striking thing is that whenever such a special science made itself independent, a parallel philosophical discipline came into being almost simultaneously. As, for example, in recent times, when formal logic separated itself from philosophy, a far reaching and hotly disputed philosophy of logic came into being. In the United States, for example, there is more discussion of this philosophy of logic than of purely logical questions, although that country leads in the field of logic, or perhaps precisely for that reason. The facts show that philosophy, instead of dying out through the development of the sciences, is becoming livelier and richer.

And finally, a nasty question for those who believe that there is no philosophy; in the name of which discipline or which science is *this* assertion made? Aristotle proposed the following to the opponents of philosophy: either, he said, one should philosophize or one should not philosophize, but if one should not philosophize then only in the name of a philosophy. Therefore, even if one shouldn't philosophize, still one must philosophize. And that is the case even today. Nothing is more amusing than the view of the supposed enemies of philosophy who introduce grandiose philosophical arguments in order to show that there is no philosophy.

The fact remains that the first opinion can be justified only with great difficulty. Philosophy must be something else than a reservoir for immature problems. Certainly it has exercised this capacity on occasion, but it is something more than that. As opposed to this, the second opinion asserts that philosophy will never disappear even if all possible sciences detach themselves from it; for it is, according to this opinion, no science. It examines the superrational, the ungraspable, that which lies above the understanding, or at least at its limits. Therefore, it has little in common with science, with the understanding. Its realm lies beyond the rational. To philosophize does not mean, therefore, to examine with reason, but rather in some other manner, more or less 'irrationally'. This is a widespread opinion today, particularly on the European continent, and it is championed by, among others, the so-called *Existenz* philosophers. A really extreme example of this direction is certainly Professor Jean Wahl, the leading philosopher of Paris, for whom there is no essential difference between philosophy and poetry. But, in this respect, even the position of the well-known *Existenz* philosopher, Karl Jaspers, is close to his. In the interpretation of Jeanne Hersch, the philosopher from Geneva, philosophy is thinking on the border between science and music; Gabriel Marcel, another *Existenz* philosopher, printed a piece of his own music in one of his philosophical books, to say nothing of the novels which some of the present day philosophers see fit to write.

This opinion is also a respectable philosophical thesis. Indeed, much can be introduced in its favor. First, in the borderline questions – and most philosophical questions are such – man, like a poet, must make use of all his powers, his emotions, will, and fantasy. Second, the basic elements of philosophy are entirely inaccessible to the understanding. One should try to grasp them, therefore, with other means, as far as possible. Third, everything related to the understanding already belongs to this or that science. Therefore, this poetic thinking which is on the border, or even beyond the border, of understanding is what is left for philosophy. We could probably present further arguments of this kind.

But numerous thinkers resist this view; among others, those who hold with Ludwig Wittgenstein's maxim: 'Whereof one cannot speak, thereon one must be silent.'[1] By talking, Wittgenstein means here rational talking, thinking. If one cannot, these opponents of poetic philosophy say, grasp something with normal human means of knowledge, that is, with the understanding, then it cannot be grasped at all. Man has only two ways of knowing something: either directly seeing the object in some way – physically or spiritually – or to infer something. But both are functions of knowing and essentially acts of the understanding. From the fact that one loves or hates something, experiences fear or nausea or something similar, follows perhaps that one feels happy or unhappy, but nothing more beyond that. Such is the view of these philosophers, and, I'm sorry to say, they laugh in the face of the followers of the other opinion and consider them dreamers, poets, men who are not serious.

I do not want to enter into a discussion of this question here for we shall have an opportunity to do so later. However, I do want to make one remark. If we look at the history of philosophy – from Thales to Merleau Ponty and Jaspers – we find again and again that the philosopher has always tried to explain reality. But to explain means to interpret rationally, with the aid of the understanding, the object to be explained. Even those who have resisted the use of the understanding in philosophy the most doggedly – as Bergson, for example – have always done it in this manner. The philosopher, so it seems at least, is one who thinks rationally, who attempts to bring clarity – that means order, which in turn means understanding – into the world and into life. Seen historically,

[1] 'Wovon man nicht sprechen kann, darüber muss man schweigen'.

that is, as what the philosophers have actually done and not as what they have said about their work, philosophy was, for the most part, a rational, a scientific activity, a doctrine, not poetry. Now and then, philosophers were also poetically talented, Plato or Saint Augustine and, if one may compare a contemporary writer with the really great thinkers, Jean Paul Sartre, who has written a few good dramas. But, with them all of this seems to have been primarily a means of communicating thoughts. In essence, philosophy has always been, as we said, a teaching, a science.

But if this is the case, then the question comes up again: a science of what? The physical world is explored by physics, the living world by biology, that of the consciousness by psychology, and society by sociology. What remains for philosophy as a science? What is its domain?

The various philosophical schools give various answers to this question. I shall list some of the more important among them.

First answer: theory of knowledge. Whereas other sciences know, philosophy investigates the possibility of knowledge itself, the presuppositions and the limits of possible knowledge. Thus, for example, Immanuel Kant and many of his successors.

Second answer: values. Every other science investigates that which *is*, philosophy investigates, however, that which *should be*. This is the answer given by, for example, the adherents of the so-called Southern German school and numerous contemporary French philosophers.

Third answer: mankind as condition and foundation of everything else. According to the champions of this opinion, everything in the real world is related, in some way, to man. This relationship is overlooked by both the natural sciences and the moral sciences (*Geisteswissenschaften*). It is this relationship, and thus man himself, which philosophy has as its object. Such is the doctrine of many *Existenz* philosophers. Fourth answer: language. 'There are no philosophical sentences, but only clarifications of sentences', as Wittgenstein said.[1] Philosophy investigates the structure of the language of the other sciences. This is the teaching of Ludwig Wittgenstein and of most logical positivists of the present day.

These are only a few of many similar views. Each of them has its arguments and is defended in a relatively convincing manner. Each of the champions of these views says that the adherents of the other views are not even philosophers at all. One should hear the deep conviction with which such judgments are made. The logical positivists, for example, are wont to brand all philosophers who don't agree with them as metaphysicians. But, according to them, metaphysics is nonsense in the strictest sense of the word. A metaphysician produces sounds, but doesn't say anything. And so it is with the Kantians; for them, everyone is a metaphysician who is not of Kant's opinion. To be sure, they don't mean by this that the others talk nonsense, just that they are outdated and non-philosophical. And I don't even need to mention the *Existenz* philosophers' contempt for all of their opponents. It is generally known.

Now, if I may express my own personal opinion, I become

[1] 'Es gibt keine Philosophischen Sätze, sondern nur Klarlegung von Sätzen.'

uneasy when confronted with this firm belief in the one or the other conception of philosophy. It seems to me very sensible to say that philosophy should be concerned with knowledge, with values, with mankind, and with its language. But why solely with these things? Has any philosopher ever proven that there are no other objects of philosophy? I would recommend, like Goethe's Mephisto, a course in logic to anyone who would assert this so that he might learn for once what a proof really is. Nothing of the kind has ever been proven. If we look around us in the world, it seems to me that it is full of unsolved questions, important questions which belong to all of the above-mentioned fields, but which aren't and can't be treated by any separate, special science. An example of such a question is the problem of law. It is certainly not a mathematical problem, for the mathematician can formulate and investigate his laws without asking himself this question. It also doesn't belong to the science of language since it is not a matter of language, but rather of something in the world or at least in thought. On the other hand, a mathematical law is also no value, it is not something which should be, but which is. Therefore, it doesn't belong to the theory of values. If one wishes to limit philosophy to any special science or to one of the disciplines which I listed, then this problem can't even be treated, for it doesn't fit in. And still it is a real and important problem.

It seems, then, that philosophy should neither be equated with the special sciences nor limited to a special field. In a certain sense, it is a universal science, its field is not restricted to something limited or particular like those of the other disciplines.

But if that is the case, then it can and does happen that philosophy concerns itself with the same objects with which the other sciences deal. How, therefore, can philosophy be differentiated from these sciences? The answer to this is that it differs both in its methods and its point of view. In its method because the philosopher does not exclude the use of *any* of the many methods of knowledge. He is not required, for example, like the physicist, to reduce everything to sensibly observed phenomena; that is, he is not limited to the empirical-reductive method. Among other things, he can also use insight into the given and much more.

On the other hand, philosophy distinguishes itself from the other sciences by its point of view. For when it takes an object into consideration, it sees it exclusively from the standpoint, so to speak, of the borderline, of the fundamental aspects. In this sense, philosophy is a science of foundations. At the point where other sciences come to a standstill, where they assume conditions without further investigation, that is where the philosopher first begins to question. The sciences know – he asks what knowledge is; the others establish laws – he asks what a law is. The average man and the politician speak about meaning and purpose, but the philosopher asks what actually should be understood by meaning and purpose. Thus, philosophy is a radical science in the sense that it gets closer to the roots of the matter than the other sciences, and that it wants to question and investigate further at that point where the others are satisfied.

It is often not very easy to say where the real borderline is between philosophy and a special science. For example, the research into the foundations of mathematics which has developed so impressively in the course of our century is most certainly philosophic research, but at the same time, it is closely connected with mathematical investigations. There are, however, some areas in which the borderline is clearly defined. There is ontology, for example, the discipline which does not deal with this or that particular, but rather with such general matters as the thing, existence, quality, and the like. Or we have the study of values as such, not as seen in the development of society, but rather in themselves. In both of these fields philosophy borders on nothing else; there is no science beside it which does or can concern itself with these objects. And ontology is assumed in the investigations of other fields which are distinguished from it by the very fact that they can know nothing about it.

This is the way philosophy has been understood by most great philosophers of all times: as science, not as poetry, not as music, but as serious, sober research. It is a universal science in the sense that it excludes no fields and uses every method which is available. It is a science of borderline questions and fundamental problems and, thus, a radical science which is not satisfied with the assumptions of the other disciplines, but rather wants to investigate further to the very roots of things.

It must also be said that it is a terribly difficult science. The task can't be easy when almost everything is questioned, when no traditional assumptions and methods are valid, when the very complicated problem of ontology must always be kept in mind. Small wonder that the opinions in philosophy are so varied. Saint Thomas Aquinas, a great thinker and no sceptic – on the contrary, one of the greatest systematicians of history – once said that only a few men, and then only after a long time and not without their share of errors, could solve the basic questions of philosophy.

But man is compelled to philosophize whether he wants to or not. I should like to say one more thing in closing. In spite of the immense difficulties which it involves, philosophizing is one of the most wonderful and noble things in human life. Whoever has met a real philosopher but once will always feel drawn to the memory of this contact.

Knowledge

AT THE CLOSE of the fifth century before Christ, there lived in Sicily a Greek philosopher named Gorgias of Leontinoi. Supposedly he formulated and skillfully defended three primary propositions: first, there is nothing; second, if there were something, we wouldn't be able to know it; third, assumed that there were something and it were knowable, we would not be able to tell anyone about it. Now, it is not certain if Gorgias himself took these assertions seriously – perhaps, as some scholars maintain, it was only a joke with him. In any case, these three propositions of his have been handed down, and since then – twenty four centuries – they challenge each one of us to reflect upon them. I am personally of the opinion that we should take this challenge seriously, regardless of how strange and weird the three propositions appear. I shall go even further; it seems to me that there is hardly anyone who has not asked himself these questions in some way at least once in his life. If that hasn't been the case with you, then it probably will be in the future. The Gorgian propositions, therefore, are most certainly important propositions.

Of course, one might think that such sceptical doubt is not to be taken seriously, and is without any real significance for life. But such is not the case. For, if one were to accept these propositions, all of the seriousness in life must disappear, everything would become deception and illusion. All meaning in life, every difference between real and false, between right and wrong, between good and evil would vanish. This is a serious matter. Furthermore, a number of reasons can be advanced which support Gorgias, and oppose our normal certainty that there are things, and knowable things in the world. It would be better to formulate the question concerning these three propositions clearly and attempt to answer it. Therefore, I should like to invite you today to reflect with me about them.

Two thousand years after Gorgias, another philosopher, the Frenchman René Descartes, reflected on these very problems. Perhaps it will be best to follow him, at least in the presentation of the reasons for doubt. We note, following Descartes, that our senses have deceived us only too often. From a distance, a rectangular tower looks round. Sometimes we believe that we hear or see something which doesn't even exist; to a sick person even sweet food sometimes tastes bitter. These are all well-known facts. Furthermore, we have dreams and often during a dream we definitely believe that the dream is reality. Now, how can we know that we are not dreaming right now? At this moment, I believe that this table, this microphone, and the bright lamps standing around me are real. But what if this were a dream?

Indeed, one can say that I can at least be certain that I have hands and feet. However, that is also not so certain as it seems to be. Thus, people who have lost a hand or a foot tell that for a long time after the amputation they feel sharp pains in the extremities which they no longer have. And modern science lends us many more arguments of the same kind; we know from psychology, for example, that from a blow on the eye the patient can see a light, a light that isn't even there. It seems to follow then that everything which surrounds us, and even our own bodies, could be mere appearance or a dream.

Now, some say that at least the mathematical truths can be known with certainty. The senses can deceive us, they say, but the understanding grasps its objects with certainty. But that too can be easily refuted. For errors can also happen in mathematics; from time to time we all make mistakes in figuring, and this happens even to the greatest mathematicians. Further, it also occurs that we occasionally count in our dreams and count falsely without noticing it. It follows that the understanding can deceive us just as well as the senses.

Is there, then, nothing certain which would not be open to doubt? Descartes believed to have found something like this in his own 'I'. He said that if I deceive myself then I must also be, for in order to think – and doubt or self-deception is surely thinking – one must exist. From this comes his famous saying: *cogito ergo sum* – I think therefore I am. Then, with the help of some rather complicated mental gymnastics, he attempts to deduce from this 'I am', the proof that other things also exist.

But most philosophers who have investigated his train of thought are not in agreement with this aspect of his system. They say, and it seems to me justifiably, that Descartes had mistaken two entirely different things: the content of thinking and the thinker himself. Of course, we all believe that for there to be any thinking, a thinker must exist. But, if one doubts everything, even the mathematical truths, then this truth will also become questionable. From the Cartesian standpoint, we have no right to assert this. For the *cogito* proves only that there is thinking, whereby the word 'is' here merely means that we have a notion of some mental content. To conclude from this the existence of a thinker is totally unjustified. A later philosopher remarked maliciously that one should not say; I think therefore I am, but rather; I think therefore I am not.

In short, we have absolutely no reason to assume anything as definitely existing. It could very well be that, as Gorgias said, there is nothing and we can know nothing. Everything would be mere appearance, a tale told by an idiot, to use Shakespeare's language.

Now, I am perfectly aware that this idiotic tale is distasteful to most of us. But this is not a question of being tasteful or distasteful. In spite of everything which has been said by certain poetic philosophers, even the greatest love cannot create its object. Whether there is something or whether there is nothing cannot be decided by wishing. One must attempt *to know*. We must attack the problem with understanding.

But how? A physicist, a botanist, a historian, and all of us in daily life assume that there *are* things, and that we can know them. But here this assumption itself is being questioned. It is one of those cases in which something more than the special sciences is necessary, a case where the role and importance of philosophy can be directly seen.

But how should we proceed? One thing is clear: a *proof*

which deduces something new from something which is already known cannot be used here. For the sceptic, like Gorgias, doubts everything, even our presuppositions. He would also doubt the rules by which we deduce. This, then, is a blind alley.

What remains? First, we can see if the sceptic doesn't contradict himself. For, if that were the case, he would actually be saying nothing consistent, nothing understandable. But that would mean that he would have said nothing.

Second, we could see if and how his assumptions stand up, whether or not they are in accord with our experience, just as the physicists do when they want to verify an hypothesis.

Finally, we could attempt to see if all of those things which Gorgias denies are *evident*, that is, whether they are as clear as we hold them to be.

The first possibility had already been explored in antiquity. If the sceptic says that one can know nothing then one can ask him how he can make such an assertion. Is the truth of his proposition certain? If so, then there *is* something certain and something knowable. Therefore, the proposition that there is nothing knowable is false. And if something is knowable then it must be, exist in some way. One tells of a Greek sceptic named Krates who realized this and therefore said nothing, instead merely moved his finger. But Aristotle, that master of European thought, remarked that he wouldn't even have any right to do that, for the movement of the finger is meant to express an opinion, and the sceptic may not have opinions. Aristotle said that he should be similar to a plant. But it is impossible to debate with a plant since it doesn't say anything.

Now, I don't know if this argumentation seems very convincing to you. However, it must be noted that mathematical logic has raised rather serious objections to it. They are based on the so-called theory of types. Unfortunately, I can't discuss this somewhat complicated theory at the moment, but I would like to warn you of too great a trust in the argument just outlined.

In contrast to this, the second possibility seems to be more reliable. If we assume that there are really things around us and that we can know them at least to a degree, then everything which we experience seems to gibe with this assumption. The difference between that which we call 'reality' and appearance consists mainly in the fact that reality is ordered, that laws hold sway in it, whereas appearance exhibits no such order. Now, we ascertain that such an order actually does reign almost everywhere in the world as we experience it. Let us take an example: I lie down in my bed and before I go to sleep I see my night-table with the alarm-clock on it. In the morning the table is still there and the clock also hasn't disappeared, in fact, there is more dust on the table than on the night before. This can best be explained if one assumes that there really is a night-table, an alarm-clock, a room, and so forth and that I know these things. Or I see a cat that appears at my left then disappears behind my back and then reappears on my right side. This can best be explained by saying that there is a real cat that continues walking behind my back. Naturally, the sceptic could say that this is all appearance, but ordered appearance. However, it is certainly simpler to assume a reality.

Finally – and this seems to me to be the best way – we can say that the falseness of Gorgias' propositions is simply self-evident. For we clearly see that something exists, some of its parts we have known with certainty and also communicated to our fellow man. But if we are told that this is all a dream, we simply answer that it is not a dream. There are instances, and many instances, in which we can err, but everyone knows of situations in which absolutely no rational doubt is possible. For example, I am now positively and absolutely certain that I am sitting and not standing, and that a lamp is burning in front of me. I am just as certain that five times eighteen is ninety. From the fact that I have erred now and then it does not follow that this must always be the case.

Therefore, I would advance the following three propositions against Gorgias: first, there exists most certainly something, second, we can definitely know some parts of it, third, it is also clear and certain that we can communicate some of the known to other men. And, as long as no one can show me a better argument than those which I find in Descartes, I see no reason to change my opinion.

Much has been gained by this, but not so much, however, as one would at first be led to believe. For, until now, we have no proof that there is a reality *outside* of our consciousness. That is a totally different and much more difficult question and one which we shall take up in our next discussion. For it could also be that there are, in fact, things and a reality, but that these are to be found only within our thinking. In this case we would also have a difference between reality and appearance, but not between the inner and the outer, however. But we shall come to that later.

Further, it does not follow from our discussion that everything which we believe to see actually *is as* we see it. *That* there is something is certain, but *how* the things in the world are constituted is another question. Many who are not sceptics believe, for example, that there are no colors in the world. But this question also does not belong in our present context, and has by no means been decided by our investigation.

Third – and this should be obvious – there exist certainly more things than we know, and we know more than we can communicate to our fellow man.

So much to avoid misunderstandings.

In this connection I would like to discuss two philosophical opinions with which I personally don't agree but which are very widespread today. On the one hand, they deal with the primacy of the 'I', and on the other hand, with the presumed necessity, in our question, of having recourse to emotional experiences.

At the present time, there are quite a few thinkers who believe that their own existence is for them more certain than anything else, or even the only entirely certain thing. Now no one – with the exception of the sceptics – will doubt that he himself really exists. But I cannot see why this should be more certain than the fact that there exists something in the world. It even seems to me that the above-mentioned sentence, *there is something*, has a certain priority over the sentence *I am*. For I know myself, so to speak, only in a roundabout way. Primarily I am directed toward the object, I grasp something in the world, perhaps badly, perhaps superficially but with the greatest certainty. The most definite truth seems to be that something exists, and primarily something which confronts me, a non-I, as the philosophers are wont to say.

Some other recent philosophers – following, it seems to me, the scholastic John Duns Scotus – think that complete certainty concerning the existence of the world and things in the world cannot be reached by mere knowledge, but rather requires so-called emotional experiences, like anxiety, fear, love or hate. In this connection, one quotes the famous description of an earthquake by the American philosopher, William James, and says that only such an experience makes mankind quite certain that there is a world. This doctrine has been developed mainly by the German thinker, Wilhelm Dilthey, who has many contemporary followers.

Somewhat similar is the popular refutation of scepticism: hit a sceptic on the head and he will quickly realize that something exists outside of himself, namely your fist. This makes sense, for who would doubt the existence of a fist which hits him. Now I don't doubt this at all but I don't see how this can help us in our question, and the same goes for an earthquake, hate, love, and so forth. For what do I experience when someone hits me on the head? First, by my sense of touch, I feel the hand, and then I experience the pain, the anger, and so forth. Now if one were to assume that the senses always decieve us, as the sceptics do, then the first point would prove absolutely nothing about the existence of the fist. And the pain and anger would prove even less, since pain or anger can be experienced without anything outside of us affecting us. Therefore, either we know that there is something through the understanding or we shall never find out by such experiences, for these already assume the validity of the act of knowledge. If this is not given then the experiences can be of no help.

The thing about scepticism is that one shouldn't make any concessions to it. For when even the smallest is made everything is quickly lost. And precisely this is done by those who deny the fact that something does confront us, as well as by those who doubt the certainty of our knowledge and would like to come to its aid by invoking fear, dread, anger, and the rest. In both cases the sceptic grasps the proffered inch and with it pulls the philosopher into his bog.

However, the fact that there is a bog and that there was a Gorgias with his three propositions is not without significance and use to the soberly thinking philosopher. Of course, what the sceptic says is highly exaggerated and thus quite simply false. But there is a kernel of truth in his exaggeration. This consists in the fact that our possibilities for knowledge are very, I would even say tragically small. We know very little and even that which we know is only too often superficial and without certainty. Most of our knowledge is only probable. *There are* indeed absolute, unconditional certainties, but these are rare. Man moves about in the world by laborious groping and trying, like a blind man, with few clear insights and very little certain success. Anyone who would believe that we know everything, know it completely, and can communicate everything that we know – such a man would be guilty of just as great and just as false an exaggeration as the sceptic.

For in philosophical questions – this is what we learn again and again in reflecting on the great problems – nothing is simple. Every simple solution is a false solution and it is usually a lazy solution, like scepticism which frees us from the duty of undertaking laborious research since, according to it, there is nothing to do research on. Reality is immensely complex and the truth about it must also be immensely complex. Only by long and painstaking work can mankind assimilate some, not much, but at least some of it.

Truth

IN OUR LAST discussion, we dealt with the question of whether or or not things exist and whether we can know them. To put it another way, we asked ourselves whether there is such a thing as truth. For correct knowledge is *true* knowledge. If one has known something then one knows that it is true to say that it is this or that. Today we would like to turn to another problem: the question, namely, what *is* truth? This old question, once asked by Pilate of Christ, is one of the most interesting, but also one of the most difficult philosophical problems.

Now, what does it mean when we say that a proposition or a judgment is true, or when we say that a person is a true friend? It is easy to see what we mean: we mean that something is true when it *obtains*. Thus, we say that John is a true friend when he is in accord with our ideal of a true friend, if it is true of him.

It is also easy to see that this *being true* can happen in two directions. In the first case, a *thing* is in accord with a thought, as when one says: this metal is true gold, or this person is a true hero. Here the thing is in accord with the thought. This first kind of *being true* and truth, the philosophers usually call 'ontological', it is the so-called ontological truth. But, in other cases, it is the other way around; the *thought*, judgment, and proposition are called true when they correspond to the thing. This second kind of *being true* has a characteristic by which it is easily recognized: in this second sense, only thoughts, judgments or propositions are true, but not things in the world. The philosophers call this second kind of *being true* 'logical truth'.

For our purposes, we can limit ourselves to this second kind and not touch upon the first which raises particularly difficult problems.

Now, what logical truth is, can be understood by using an example. Let us take the statement: 'The sun is shining today.' This statement – and thus the corresponding thought – is then true if and only if the sun is really shining today. It can be deduced from this that a statement and a proposition are then logically true when things actually are as they say they are. If things are other than as they say, then they are false. This seems to be clear and obvious. And still the matter is by far not so simple as one at first might think. For it is related to two serious and difficult problems.

The first problem can be presented in the following manner: If a proposition is then true when things are as it says they are, then it must unconditionally be true or false always, regardless of who says it or when it is said. To put it differently, when a proposition is true, it is *absolutely* true for all men and for all times.

At this point various doubts arise. Some of these are so weighty that some philosophers and even some non-philosophers are wont to say that truth is relative, conditional, changeable, and so forth. The French even have a saying which goes: 'True this side of the Pyrenees, false on the other

43

side.' And today it has almost become the fashion to maintain that the truth is relative. Now what are the reasons for such a conception?

Some of these reasons are superficial and can be easily refuted. It is said, for example, that the proposition 'it is raining today', is only relatively true because it is raining in Rome but not in Munich. Therefore, this proposition is true in Rome but false in Munich. And then there is the Indian story of the two blind men, one of whom grasps the leg of an elephant and says that it is like a tree, whereas the other grasps the trunk and maintains that it is like a snake.

All of these are misunderstandings. It is enough to formulate these propositions completely, to say clearly what is meant, in order to realize that this has nothing to do with relativity. When someone says that it is raining today, he obviously means that it is raining here in Munich on a certain day and at a certain hour, but not that it is raining everywhere. His proposition is therefore unconditionally true for all times and for all peoples. Neither does the experience of the blind men with the elephant prove anything against the unconditional character of truth. They merely expressed themselves carelessly. Had each of them said: 'the elephant is similar to a tree in respect to that extremity which I touched, and so forth', then the proposition would have been unconditionally true. The difficulty here arises from an inadequate formulation of the propositions. Once these are clearly expressed, it becomes evident that they are unconditionally true or unconditionally false, and not at all relative.

But we know of even more serious doubts concerning the unconditionality of truth. Contrary to popular opinion, there are today not only one but several geometries. Beside that of Euclid, which is taught in the schools, there are also geometries of Rieman, Lobatschewsky, and still others. And the fact is that certain propositions which are true in one of these geometries are false in another. Therefore, if we ask a present day geometrician whether a certain proposition is true or false he first must ask: in which system? The geometric propositions are, to a great degree, relative to the system.

Worse still, the same holds true for logic. There are also different systems in logic, so that the question whether a certain logical proposition is true or not cannot be answered without reference to a definite system. For example, the well-known law of the excluded middle – that it rains or it doesn't rain – is valid in the so-called classical logic of Whitehead and Russell, but invalid in the logic of Professor Heyting. In this sense, the truth of logical propositions is therefore relative.

Now, one might think that there must be a way to decide among all of these systems which one is right, whether it is valid or not. But things aren't that simple. For example, if we take the case of geometry then the experts tell us that the Euclidian holds up well in our small world, but that, in outer space, another one is more consistent with the facts. Therefore, a proposition would be true under certain circumstances but false under others. This is indeed a serious problem.

Let us assume that things are as these experts tell us, that, in the realm of mathematics and logic, there are various systems, and that certain propositions can be true in one and false in another. Then the question immediately arises: what leads us to choose the one and not the other among these systems? Surely it isn't purely arbitrary. A physicist, Einstein, for example, did not choose a certain geometry because he felt like it, he had serious reasons for his choice. Which reasons? The answer to this is of great philosophical importance. The answer is that the scientists and mankind in general do not consider a proposition or system true because it is in accord with reality, but rather because it is *useful*. A physicist, for example, chooses a non-Euclidian geometry because, with it, he can develop his theories and explain reality, or at least do this better and more easily.

But, if that is the case, then those propositions are called true which are useful. Truth is utility, it is said. That is the so-called pragmatic concept of truth which was developed, above all, by William James, the famous and beloved American thinker, and which today has many adherents.

This doctrine has this to say for it: there are certainly sectors of the sciences in which we assume propositions only because they are useful for further research or for the construction of theories. But two things should be noticed here. First, in such cases we don't really know if the respective propositions are true or false; they are merely useful. And it is difficult to see why one should call this utility truth and speak of the relativity of truth. Second, even when we are dealing with utility we cannot get around knowing at least some *true* propositions, and I mean 'true' in the usual sense of the word. For example, a physicist establishes a theory and believes it to be useful; how can he prove this? Only by testing it against the facts. But that again means that he sets up certain propositions which should be verified by direct observation. Later, in some laboratory, a scientist writes the following sentence, for example: 'Under such and such conditions, the pointer of the ammeter pointed to such and such today, at ten hours, twenty minutes and fifteen seconds.' Now, this last sentence is then true only when it actually applies, only when the pointer of the ammeter actually did point there and nowhere else at that time and under those circumstances. Therefore, even as a pragmatist, one must admit that there are certain true propositions in the Aristotelian sense; the rest, however, should not be called 'true', but simply 'useful.'

So much for the first question. Let us now turn to the second, which is: what is this something with which the proposition should agree in order to be true? One might think that the situation is very clear. In order to be true, the proposition must agree with the *way things are*, with the condition of things as they are outside of us. But this too is problematical. Let us take, for example, the sentence: 'this rose is red'.

Should we assert that this proposition is then true if the rose is really red, then we are told that in the external world there isn't any redness, for colors come to be only in our organs of sight as the result of the effect of certain light waves that strike our eyes. There is no such thing as an external color, we are taught by our physiologists. Therefore, it can't be right that our sentence is only then true when it agrees with the external state of affairs, for such a state doesn't exist. *What*, then, must a proposition agree with in order to be true?

This and similar doubts have led numerous modern thinkers to acknowledge a philosophical doctrine which is called 'epistemological idealism'. According to it, there are indeed things and unconditional truths, but all of these are not outside of us. In one way or another, they are *in us*, in our thinking. Naturally the question immediately arises as to how true propositions and real things can be differentiated from false propositions and pure imagination. But the idealists answer that the difference exists also from their point of view. Everything we know is a product of our thinking, is *in us;* we produce some of these objects according to *laws*, others arbitrarily. That was basically the teaching of the great German philosopher, Immanuel Kant, which today is followed by some, but not many, philosophers.

In order to portray this doctrine somewhat better, let us return to the example of the cat. The cat comes from my left, goes behind my back, thereby disappearing for a while, then reappears on my right side and moves on. In the last discussion I said that the matter can be explained best by saying that an 'external' cat goes behind my back. The idealists cannot admit of such a cat because, for them, there is no externality in the strict sense of the word. But they say that the cat is in so far actual as it is thought of by me *in accordance with laws*. It is, therefore, not a figment of my imagination but actuality. Furthermore, the entire space which the cat and I occupy, my own body and so forth, are also actual, that is, thought of according to laws.

There are, therefore, *two* possible interpretations of truth – the idealistic and the *realistic*, as the other is called. Both involve great difficulties, and to decide for one or the other is certainly no easy task. I should like to point out to those who believe that idealism is simply nonsense that they haven't understood it at all. It would be nonsense to deny reality and the truth, but the idealists by no means do that.

Most contemporary philosophers, however, are not idealists. Their decision against this conception of the truth and of knowledge in general usually occurs while reflecting on the question of what human knowledge really is. According to idealism, one must say that knowledge is *creative*, it *creates* its objects. Now, it is obvious that our personal, individual thoughts can create only very little, at the most products of the imagination which consist mostly of elements which are not created anew but only rearranged among themselves, as, for example, when I think of a siren. This siren consists of a half of a lady and a half of a fish; in order to have created a siren I must have seen both of these somewhere. This is certain and obvious.

Therefore, the idealists are forced to assume a twofold subject, twofold thought, a double I: the little, personal I – this they call the empirical I – and a big, superpersonal, *transcendental* I, or the I 'in general'.

But their opponents, the realists, say that all of this is very problematical and hardly believable. What is this transcendental I which is actually no longer an I, but which hovers above me, so to speak? An absurdity, say the realists. Such a thing doesn't exist and is even hard to imagine. Further, if we examine our activity of knowing more closely it becomes obvious that it combines, unites, and perhaps even now and then creates different things in it, but mainly it consists in our *comprehending* an object which, in some way, is already there and is external to our activity of knowing.

Now, the conflict between idealism and realism is a conflict concerning the conception of knowledge: does it consist in creating or grasping an object? If one should decide for the idealistic solution then one must struggle with truly enormous difficulties. It is much better, so say the realists, to stick to the first opinion, particularly since it seems to reproduce the nature of knowledge better.

Of course, the realistic conception also has its serious difficulties. One I have already mentioned: it is the difficulty which stems from the scientifically proven fact that there seem to be no colors in the world. At least in this instance, it seems as if we had created something by our knowledge: colors. Let us see what answer the realists have to this difficulty.

Their answer is twofold. First, they say that the borderline between the knower and the outer world is not the human epidermis. It is to be found wherever the transition between the physical and the psychic takes place. What the mind comprehends are the events as they reveal themselves in the organism. If we wear red glasses then green objects appear black; however, no one would maintain that we have created this black color through our activity of knowing. On the contrary, it is the result of the effect of the glasses. It is similar with our eyes.

Second, the realists maintain that, in many cases, we do not comprehend the things in themselves but the things *acting upon us*, that is, we comprehend the relationship between the things and our body. As, for example, when we put our right hand in hot water, the left in cold, and then both in luke warm water. We then feel coldness in the right and warmth in the left. That is clear, say the realists, for our sense of temperature registers the difference between the temperature of the skin and that of the outer world. But this sense *registers* and does not create the temperature. It is *given*.

Another, somewhat more subtle difficulty which the idealists often raise is that that which is known must be *within* the activity of knowledge, and therefore not outside; thus we may not speak of an 'external'. But the realists answer that this is both a misunderstanding and superstition. Here, knowing is being conceived as if it were a box; a thing must either be inside or outside of the box. Now, knowledge is certainly not a box. It can best be compared, as Edmund Husserl has done, to a source of light: when a ray of light falls on a thing in the dark this thing is in the light but still not within the source of light.

Years ago, after much struggle, I myself decided for realism, and the more I think about it, the more I am convinced that this conception of the truth is the right one. I know that not everyone will do the same, for the question is difficult. But regardless of what others will accept as solutions, I want to warn you of *one* misunderstanding. In this question, one's decision must be *uncompromising*. *All* of human knowledge must be understood either as a comprehending or as a creating of the object. Every compromise is false, as, among others, the popular one according to which we would have forms and light waves in the outer world, but no colors. One must maintain either that there is no external world at all and that our mind creates everything or, on the contrary, that it creates nothing beside the combination of contents, and that everything which we know must be present, in some way, outside of the mind.

An important German psychologist, Fechner, once wrote an article in which he contrasted the day-world with the night-world, a world in which there would be no colors, no sounds, merely mechanical movements and forms in the dark. He decidedly rejected this night view. It will perhaps interest you to know that most present day philosophers share his view; that is, they are *for* a world of light and against the dark view we have described.

Thinking

IT IS TO THINKING, much more than to observation, that we owe the impressive accomplishments of our science. It is on the point of reshaping the face of the earth and the structure of our life. It will certainly be worthwhile to reflect a little on this process of thinking. What actually is it? How is it possible that it helps us to get to know something? How is it formed, which ways does it go in scientific research? And finally, the most important question: what is its value? Can we trust it, believe in its results, permit it to lead us through scientific thinking? Today, I would like to discuss briefly some of these weighty questions with you.

First, what is thinking? Quite generally, every movement in our ideas, concepts, and so forth is called thinking. For example, when someone asks me: 'What are you thinking of', I answer, 'I am thinking of my family'. But this means that images, memories, and such somehow are present and follow one another in my consciousness. Therefore, the most common definition of thinking is a movement of ideas and concepts.

But scientific thinking is not any ordinary thinking. It is *serious* thinking. We mean by this that it is *disciplined* thinking, that a seriously thinking man does not give his ideas and concepts the freedom simply to hover in his mind, but rather directs them toward his goal. Further, we mean that the goal here is *knowledge*. Scientific, serious thinking is thinking which is disciplined and directed toward knowledge.

But how can such thinking become knowledge for us? One might think that the object which we want to know is either there, given, thus needing no thinking to see it but merely opening one's eyes or directing one's attention to it, or that this object is absent, not given, and in this case – so it seems at least – thinking about it cannot bring it any closer.

And yet this is not the case. We need only to call upon our experience to see that thinking can play a useful, often decisive role in both cases.

First, let us consider the case in which the object is given. This object is never completely simple. Usually it is very, almost infinitely complex. It has hundreds of sides, aspects, characteristics, and so forth. But our mind is not in the position to grasp all of this at one time. In order to get to know such an object well, one must diligently look at one side after the other, compare what has been seen, and always consider and analyze the matter from new standpoints. But all of this is *thinking*.

Let us take an example of such thinking. Suppose that a red dot is here before my eyes. At first, one might imagine that this is very simple, and all that has to be done is to open one's eyes in order to see what it is. But a red dot is not so simple; for there can't be any red dot at all when there is no background to it, and the color of the background must be different than the color of the dot. This is the first point. Second, we can ascertain a rather simple but still remarkable fact:

the dot must not only have a color but also *dimensions*, a definite length and width. But these dimensions are not a color, they are something completely different, although they are necessarily connected with the color. Third, these dimensions alone are still not enough. The dot must have a shape, a form – it can be square or round, for example, but it must have some form. If we consider it further, we find that its color is also no simple matter; indeed it is a red color but not just any red color, rather a very definite shading, nuance. If there are two dots, then usually the tone or shading will not be the same. In analyzing the color one can, in fact, go a great deal further. As anyone knows who has studied the theory of colors, the intensity of the color can also be discussed, for example. If we note further that the dot appears not only on a differently colored background but also on something, on a carrier, then we have discovered no less than seven elements in it: background, color, dimension, shape, tone, intensity, and finally the carrier. And this is just the beginning.

But this is a very simple, trivial example. If we were dealing with mental objects like 'pardon' or 'talent', then one can imagine what truly infinite complexity is to be found in these, and how great the work of thinking must be in order to get one's self oriented to some degree.

In history, this kind of thinking has always been applied by the philosophers. The great master of it was Aristotle. At the beginning of this century, a leading German philosopher, Edmund Husserl, considerably clarified and trenchantly described this method. He called it 'phenomenological'. Phenomenology is – at least in the early writings of Husserl –

a method through which we attempt to grasp the essence of the given object by an analysis similar to the one presented above.

But in the natural sciences this kind of thinking plays a subordinate role. There the main emphasis is on another kind of thinking, namely, thinking which attempts to grasp the *non-given*, the absent object, so to speak. Such thinking is also called reasoning.

In this connection, I should like to make a very important remark. As I have already said, there are only *two* possible alternatives: either the object is *given* or it isn't. If it is given then it should simply be seen and described; but if it isn't given, then we have *only one* possibility to find out something about it, namely reasoning. There is no third way to knowledge. Naturally, one can believe in something, but belief is not knowledge. We can know only by observation of the given or by reasoning.

This point should be stressed because, in our day, there exist various and widespread misunderstandings. It is said, for example, that one can get to know something by good or bad intentions. Others maintain that a leap of freedom or something similar is an instrument of knowledge. Now, of course, one can imagine that the leaping could be useful as a preparation for the act of knowing. For example, if I want to know a cow that is standing behind a wall then a leap over the wall can lead to my knowing it. But after I have courageously made this leap I still must open my eyes, and only by looking will I learn something about the cow. No leap of freedom or anything similar can be *more* than a *preparation* for the act of knowing. But this is always, as we said, either a direct grasping of the object – that is, a sensory or a mental comprehension – or a reasoning.

Now, reasoning presents numerous difficult problems. The most important of these problems reads: how is it at all possible to discover or get to know a non-given object by an inference? I must admit that this problem seems very difficult to me, and I don't know of a complete solution. But one thing is certain; we *can* learn something by deduction. The following example will clearly show this. If I am asked how much twenty three thousand, one hundred and sixty nine times seven thousand, eight hundred and forty seven is, at first I don't know. But if I sit down and go through the multiplication then I know that it is one hundred and eighty one million, eight hundred and seven thousand, one hundred and forty three. But multiplying is thinking, it is reasoning. Therefore, whoever maintains that a result can be known without it, without figuring, should tell me *how*; I would be very thankful to him. But in case he can't tell me that then he must admit that I have learned something by reasoning. It cannot be seriously doubted that we even learn by it all the time.

But how does reasoning take place? Without exception, we always have two things as conditions: on the one hand, certain premises, that is, statements or propositions which are either known as true or accepted in some way and, on the other hand, some *rule* by which we infer. For example, in order to deduce that the street is wet I can have the premises: 'if it rains then the street is wet', and 'it is raining'. Beside this I must know the rule which the logicians call *modus ponendo ponens* which roughly reads: when there is a conditional sentence – a sentence which begins with an 'if' – and its antecedent, then its consequent can be accepted. The ancient Stoics formulated this rule in the following way: If the first, then the second; but the first, therefore the second. Logic, or more precisely formal logic, is the science which investigates such rules.

But there are two completely different types of such rules. First, there is a great number of rules which are *infallible*, that means that, if these rules are correctly applied, the result is positively certain. An example of such a rule is precisely our *modus ponendo ponens*. Another example is the well-known mode of syllogism by which one deduces that if all logicians are mortal, and Lord Russell is a logician then Lord Russell is also mortal. Second, there are very many rules which are *not infallible*. And the troublesome thing in life and in science is that these fallible rules play a much greater role than the infallible ones.

This matter is so important that we must concern ourselves with it a little more closely. The fallible rules are all basically certain conversions of our *modus ponendo ponens*. In this, one infers from the antecedent to the consequent, that is, from the first the second. That is an infallible rule. But in the other kind of rules, one follows an inverted scheme: if the first then the second; but the second; therefore the first. That this is no infallible rule can be seen when one infers, for example, in the following way: if I am Napoleon then I am a man; now, I am a man, therefore I am Napoleon. Here both premises are true but the conclusion is false, for I am unfortunately not Napoleon. Therefore, the rule is not infallible. The logicians would even say that it is false.

But in life, and particularly in science, we almost always infer in this way. So-called induction, for example, consists completely in such inference. For in induction we have as premise that some individuals behave so or so. On the other hand, we know from logic that when all individuals behave so and so then *some* will also behave the same way; from this we can conclude that *all* individuals behave so or so. An example: the chemists have determined that some pieces of phosphorous burn at, let us say, forty-two degrees centigrade; they conclude from this that *every* piece of phosphorous burns at forty-two degrees. The train of thought is the following: if all burn then these few will also burn; but since these few burn, then all will burn. Precisely as in the case of Napoleon, it is a conclusion from the second to the first. It is a non-infallible conclusion.

Of course, the train of thought in science is not as simple as we have portrayed it here. Quite the contrary. Mankind has found many, highly refined methods of reinforcing its non-infallible conclusions. But all of this only slightly changes the basic fact that all of natural science proceeds by non-infallible rules. The result is that the theories of natural science are never completely certain truths. Everything which science can and actually does attain in this respect is probability.

And even with this probability things aren't quite so simple as some perhaps believe. For, first of all, we don't know even today what the probability of these hypotheses really is. It seems that it must be something quite different from, for example, the probability of an automobile accident which can be calculated. This can be seen from the following: most laws of modern physics are laws of probability, that is, they merely state that an event will happen with a certain probability. But these laws about probability are, evidently in another sense, themselves probable.

But even if we knew what probability is, we would still have to answer the question: how can we attain probability at all? That we can determine one is certain, but up until now we don't know *how* this is possible.

Now, I am aware that all of these doubts will seem unfounded to you in view of the great successes of science. But please tell me what reason you have to assume that the sun is going to rise tomorrow? You will most likely answer that it has always been that way. But this reason is not sufficient. For years my aunt's cat came into her room every morning through the window; but one day it came no more. When it is said that the laws of nature are uniform then I ask *how* we know this. Solely because we have observed this uniformity up until now, as in the case of the sun or the cat? It can by no means be concluded from this that they will be just as uniform tomorrow.

These considerations permit us to take a clearer position towards science. The principles of this position could be formulated in the following way:

First, from the practical standpoint, science – if it is *real* science – is definitely the best thing which we have. It is highly useful.

Second, even seen theoretically, we hardly have anything better when dealing with the explanation of nature. Science supplies, in addition to sentences about observed phenomena, only probable statements. In this respect, however, we can attain nothing more anywhere else.

Third, it follows from this that the thinking man should declare himself for science and against any other human authority when it comes to a contradiction between them. This is particularly true for the so-called ideologies; that is, assertions which are made on the basis of some human, social or other authority. For this reason, practically all the philosophers of the world reject and condemn the Communist ideology which opposes propositions of Marx, Engels, and Lenin to science. This is irrational and inadmissible.

Fourth, since science, for the most part, supplies only probable propositions, it can happen that they may be rejected by calling on that which is immediately self-evident. Science is not infallible, and if we have encountered something which is self-evident and opposed to that which science maintains then we may and should decide in favor of that which is self-evident and be against the scientific theories.

Fifth, science is competent only in *its own* realm. Unfortunately, it often happens that even important scientists assert things which don't have the slightest thing to do with their field. A classical and crass example of such a trespassing of the limits of competence is that famous assertion of a learned doctor who said that there couldn't be a human consciousness because he had dissected so many bodies and had never found one. The inconsistency here is that the science of this doctor, due to its own methods, is limited to the research of *bodies*, and the consciousness is most definitely not a body; quite apart from the fact that the bodies which the doctor had dissected were dead. However, if we look at this example a little more closely we find the following: the good doctor had absolutely no scientific basis or reason for making such an assertion.

In order to legitimate it, he had to presuppose that only bodies exist in this world. That is, however, not natural science, nor surgery, but pure, although bad, philosophy.

And this is precisely the great danger. Enormous areas of reality have not yet been investigated, nor even made accessible to exact scientific research – particularly if we are dealing with man. Even where research is underway we know unbelievably little. What now happens is that man wants to fill the enormous gaps in scientific knowledge with his private, grossly naive, and false philosophy which is then proclaimed as science. This is done not only by some scientists but by many other men. Science, however, enjoys such a great authority that, in this respect, its representatives are the most dangerous when they begin to philosophize beyond their competence.

Thus, for this reason, if society allows itself the luxury of having a few philosophers, although these philosophers don't help to produce airplanes or atom bombs, perhaps it really does make good sense. For philosophy, and philosophy alone, can warn of the madness which, due to false thinking, often threatens us under the supposed authority of science. In one of its most important functions, philosophy is nothing more than the defense of true thinking against fantasy and nonsense.

Values

GOETHE, one of the greatest poets mankind has ever had, often ridiculed theory and speculation. 'Gray, my friend, is all your theory', and you know well the passage where he says: 'a man to speculation bound is like a senseless beast upon a barren heath by evil spirit led in circles round and round . . .' I am of the opinion that he, and with him all poets and perhaps all women, who generally think like poets, is right when he rejects exaggerating theoretical thinking. For man does not merely contemplate reality. He not only *sees* it, he also *evaluates* it; he finds this reality agreeable or hateful, good or evil, pleasant or unpleasant, noble or common, sacred or profane and so on. We are so made that we can rise to a purely observant attitude only by great effort and then only in rare moments. By and large, our life is determined by evaluating and values.

Given this fact, it can of course be asked: why then all of this philosophizing and reflection? Let us plunge into the life of values! Goethe opposed the eternally green tree of life to gray theory. Many present day philosophers also think this way, among others, Gabriel Marcel, who established the basic rule: you are not in a theater, that is, you should live, not observe. It seems to me that thinking, pure observing, is also a part of life and that Goethe's contrast between life and theory is wrong. It seems to me that a full human life without at least some moments of pure theory, of pure contemplation, is no human life at all. But contemplation is certainly not everything in this life, and also not everything which makes it a *human* life. Values and all that goes with them are just as essential a part of this life as theories.

For this reason, the philosopher must deal with values. Actually, the theory of values, the attempt to clarify this side of our lives, has been a basic part of every philosophy for thousands of years; this, if for no other reason, because, among all the other realms, the realm of values presents the greatest difficulties. Regardless of how simple and clear values seem to be to our minds, the situation becomes terribly complex when we attempt to understand them correctly.

Let us begin with an example. I hope that I will be excused for offering such a very crass and crude example, but we are not dealing here with feelings but with the understanding, and such crude examples clarify better than anything else the nature of that which is being examined. The example is the following: A delinquent youth, we'll call him Jack, advises his friend Tom to take a razor blade out of the drawer during the night, cut his sleeping mother's throat, and then steal her money. The money would then be used by the two boys for a good time at a bar. Tom, assuming that he is a normal human being, replies with indignation that he would never do such a thing. Jack then asks why not, it would be so simple and so useful. What can Tom answer to this? Let us put ourselves in his position. What would *we* say or answer? I fear that we wouldn't be able to find the right answer. Perhaps we would say that it is criminal, base, something forbidden, dirty, sinful and so forth. But if Jack were to ask us why one should not do something criminal, dirty or sinful we would only be able to answer that such things just aren't done. In other words, we would have no answer. We could not give a reason or proof for our position. The sentence 'you should not cut your mother's throat in order to get money for drinking' cannot be proven. It is *self-evident;* the most that can be said is that things just *are* this way and that we cannot discuss it further.

Such, therefore, is our situation. Let us now attempt to analyse it a bit in order to find out what components make up this complex situation. We shall apply the phenomenological method described in our last discussion since, for this object, there is no other.

First, we ascertain that our sentence 'you should not kill your mother and so on' seems to all of us to be *given*. It is there, in our minds, something completely independent of us, existing in itself, just like an object in the world, only perhaps more solid than the simple things. It is, as the philosophers say, a being. What kind of being? Obviously it is no real being. In the world such a *thing* doesn't exist; the sentence is also valid beyond time and place. It is ideal being, of the same kind as mathematical forms.

But, and this is a big difference, it is not simply there as a mathematical formula is. Such a formula merely says what *is*, whereas our sentence *demands;* it says what *should* be. It stands before our conscience like a summons, a commandment. This is quite remarkable, but it is nonetheless the case.

Third, this commandment, this sentence is, as Kant once remarked, *categorical*. This means that it is meaningless to ask *why* I should act in such a manner. In technology it is a different matter. For example, in the technique of driving a car there is the following command: 'one should give gas approximately two-thirds of the way through the curve'. This command is hypothetical, that means that it depends on a purpose, for it is valid only in so far as we want to navigate the curve quickly and safely. If we didn't want to do this then the command would lose its meaning. But it is completely different with our sentence about the mother. It is *categorical*. It demands *unconditionally*, without consideration of any purpose. Should the earth burst if I don't kill my mother it would still obtain that I may not murder her.

Fourth – but only fourth – we note that the insight into such a commandment, such a sentence, directly *acts upon us*. The clearer it is, the stronger is our reaction, the more intense our will, our indignation or our enthusiasm. Naturally, this reaction is also dependent on our momentary physical and mental condition – if I am tired then my reaction is weakly – but primarily it is determined by the object and by our insight into this object.

So much for the description of the situation. Let us now turn to an explanation of this remarkable and important phenomenon. I should like to preface this explanation with a short remark about the different concepts and kinds of values which will appear here.

In view of what has been said, three things must be sharply distinguished: first, a *thing*, something real which is valuable – either positively or negatively – for example, good or bad. In our case, this reality is the act of murder. This reality, is characterized by a quality which makes it evaluable.

This quality, and this is the second point, is called *'value'*, in the most exact sense of the word. Third, there is, as we remarked, our relations and reactions to it, our insight into values, our will, which either desires something or becomes indignant about something and so forth. These three things should not be confused for they are totally different: the object of the value, the value itself, and the human attitude toward the value.

If it is a question of the values themselves, then there are at least three large groups of such values in the realm of mind. These are called moral, aesthetic, and religious. The moral values are best known; they are characterized by a demand *for action,* they always contain a 'should do' and not only a 'should be', like all other values. Aesthetic values – those of beauty, ugliness, elegance, coarseness, nobleness, tenderness, sublimeness and so forth – are also well known. They are characterized by a 'should be' but no 'should do'. If, for example, one sees a beautiful building then one also sees that it *should be* as it is, but this value does not involve, at least directly, an appeal to our conscience. And lastly, there are the religious values which are perhaps of a completely different nature. They are also well known to religious people, and each of us is, in some way, more or less religious. But the analysis of these values is very difficult. It is certain that they spread a feeling of awe and at the same time self-surrender in us which, in some way, is connected with a tremendous number of aesthetic and moral reactions. But they appear to belong neither to the moral nor to the aesthetic values. The murder of one's mother is, for example, a crime from the moral standpoint, an evil deed; but from the religious standpoint it is something completely different, namely a *sin*. The moral values have been investigated the most by philosophers, the aesthetic values have been analysed much less and the religious are still awaiting a basic examination. The deceased Louis Lavelle, a leading French philosopher, wrote a very good book about this – it is called 'The Four Saints' – but even he didn't carry the analysis very far.

Now for the explanations. At the center of the discussion is the question concerning the interpretation of change in valuation. One might think that valuation is constant, that, for example, our sentence about the mother is recognized at all times and places. But this is not the case. Moral valuation – and even more so the aesthetic and religious – is very different at different times and in different cultures. Malinowski, a Polish ethnologist who did research in Australia, once wrote a positively frightening book about the sexual morals of the natives there. Reading this book, one gets the impression that practically everything which we consider valid and even perhaps holy is seen as evil and criminal somewhere else. As for aesthetic values, it is well known that women whom we consider ugly are held to be extremely beautiful by certain negro races. Valuation, therefore, seems to be highly relative. Now, there are primarily two basic philosophical theories which attempt an interpretation of this state of affairs. On the one hand, the positivistic, on the other, the idealistic, idealistic in the broadest sense of the word.

The first, propounded mainly by the British empiricists, maintains that the relativity and change of valuation is to be interpreted by precisely the relativity and the change of the values themselves. Values are, according to these thinkers, nothing more than a kind of sediment of valuation. Man has become accustomed, for this or that reason – mainly reasons of utility – to evaluate in such and such a manner and then form the corresponding values. If the situation changes and the respective things and actions become useless, then the values will also change. In applying this interpretation to our example, the positivists maintain that the murder of one's mother would be socially harmful in *our* culture; for first, the mother is needed to rear the child and, second, perhaps she can have more children. But one could imagine a culture in which it would be otherwise, let us say a culture in which the children would be reared exclusively in state institutions, or even, as in Aldous Huxley's famous novel, where they would be synthetically produced in special factories where the mother, as such, wouldn't be needed. In such a culture our sentence possibly wouldn't be valid since it would no longer be useful. In such a case, Jack's suggested murder of the mother could be morally good. So much for the positivists. Of course, they also maintain that values are *real things,* that is, certain attitudes of man.

The idealists, however, feel hardly affected by these arguments. They admit that our valuation changes and that much which is considered good here is bad somewhere else. But they note that this is so not only in the case of values. The ancient Egyptians, for example, had a formula for the calculation of the surface of the triangle which is obviously false from the standpoint of our geometry. They used this formula for hundreds of years. Does this prove that there are two correct formulas for the calculation of the surface of a triangle? By no means, say the idealists. This proves only that man at that time had not yet found the right formula. The case is exactly the same for the realm of values, for valuation – our insight into the values and our reaction to them – is something completely different than the values themselves. Valuation is changeable, relative, always differing, but the values themselves are eternal and unchangeable. If the idealists are asked what basis they have for this assertion they answer us just like Tom answered Jack: 'It is self-evident.' Once one realizes what a mother is, then there can be no doubt that matricide is and always will be a crime. Whoever denies this is blind in this respect. There are value blind people just as there are color blind people.

This doctrine, which essentially stems from Plato, has been admirably developed in our century by the greatest moralist of modern times, the German philosopher, Max Scheler. Everyone who deals with these questions should have read Scheler; he may then reject him, but to speak about values without knowing this great thinker is, in my opinion, inadmissible.

Max Scheler and the other idealistic philosophers stress again and again that, in the realm of valuation, the element of change is much more preponderant than in any other theoretical realm. This can be attributed to the fact that the realm of values is of very great scope and no individual man can exhaust it; indeed no individual man can completely comprehend even *one single* value. When Christ says in the gospel that no one is good except God what is meant, among other things, is that only an infinite being, an infinitely holy spirit, can completely comprehend any value. We men see them only in fragments, always superficially, always from one side. This is a doctrine which is of huge practical importance for life. This means that there are no two men who have the same insight into a value; one sees one value – say the value of bravery – more clearly, whereas another sees another value – the value of benevolence or purity, for example – more clearly. And from this it follows that we shouldn't condemn someone as crazy if we don't understand his behaviour. He may be a hero, a saint, a genius. Unfortunately, the understanding of this truth is not very widespread, and the best of us, those who had the clearest insights into values, were condemned regularly by the mass of blind men. But yet the progress of mankind is dependent precisely on these better, clearer seeing men.

This is, however, just one side of this change. The thing about values is that insight is dependent not only on talent but above all on the will. A very decent man sees much clearer than a less decent man, for, in this realm, he sees the rightness or wrongness of a deed more clearly. Thus it happens that a man who is much more learned and talented than another stands far behind him in the particular realm of values; in fact, he is sometimes a complete barbarian in this respect.

Such is the great conflict between the positivists and the idealists. Now I shall tell you what I personally think. I am of the opinion that positivism is not tenable; it seems to me that it consists of a confusion between valuation and values, our view and reaction to the values and the values themselves. All of the facts to which positivism appeals can just as well be interpreted from the idealistic standpoint; furthermore, idealism isn't forced – as positivism is – to deny the immediate self-evidence of values. That is the first point.

Connected with this is the fact that I see values as something ideal. They are not parts or products of our mental activity. However, I would also not place values in some platonic heaven. They exist only in our minds, just like mathematical laws. In the world there are only individual things, real individual things. However, and this is the third point, there is in the world a certain foundation for values. What is this foundation? Personally, I can see here only one possible answer: values are based in the relationship between man and the things. Why, for example, is there such a thing as the value of parental love? Because the human physical and spiritual constitution is such that the child must love and obey the parents in order to prosper as a human being. Were the human constitution otherwise then we would have another aesthetics and another morality. Does it follow from this that values are changeable? Yes and no. Yes in so far as man himself is changeable. No in so far as he reveals a fixed fundamental constitution. But it happens that both of these characteristics apply: the details change but the foundation remains constant. Therefore, the fundamental values are unchangeable. As long as man remains man, no one, not even God, can change this; he will always consider matricide a crime. Only it does happen that man is blind to certain values. With this observation we have approached the border between theoretical philosophy, which seeks only to understand, and the practical, which teaches what is to be done. In closing, let me indicate a truth of this practical philosophy which seems to me to be central for human life: the light, the understanding of values, and the strength to realize them are the things which we should strive for most in this life.

Man

LET US NOW reflect on man. In this realm there are so many philosophical problems that we couldn't even begin to name them all here. Our discussion, therefore, will necessarily refer only to a few of them. Mainly we want to ask the question – along with the great thinkers of the past and of our time – what *is* man? What am I really?

It will be best, as always, if we begin by determining those qualities of man which are not subject to doubt. These can be listed under two main headings: first, man is an animal; second, he is a peculiar, quite unique animal.

He is, therefore, primarily an animal and has all of the characteristics of an animal. He is an organism, has sense organs, he grows, nourishes and moves himself, and has strong drives – the drives for self-preservation and struggle, the sexual drive, and many more, just like the other animals. If we compare man with the higher animals we see that he is definitely one type among other animal types. Of course, poets have often praised human feelings in beautiful language. But I know some dogs whose feelings, it seems to me, are much more beautiful and deeper than those of some men. Perhaps it is unpleasant but it must be admitted that we belong to the same family and that, for example, dogs and cows are something like our younger brothers and sisters. To see this we don't have to refer to the theory of evolution, according to which man stems, to be sure not from the apes as is often said, but still from an animal. That he is an animal is obvious even without any learned zoology.

He is, however, a remarkable animal. Much is peculiar to him which we find only faint traces of, if at all, in the other animals. What is most striking about this is that man, from the biological point of view, has absolutely no right to impose himself on the entire animal world, to dominate it and, as the greatest parasite of nature, to profit from it the way he does. He is an animal that has turned out badly. Bad eyes, almost no sense of smell worth mentioning, inferior hearing: these are most certainly his characteristics. He lacks natural weapons, like claws, almost completely. His strength is minimal. He can neither run nor swim fast. Besides this, he is naked and dies much more easily from cold, heat, and similar things than most animals. Biologically seen, he has no right to existence. He should have perished long ago, like so many other inferior animals.

And yet things have turned out quite differently. Man is the master of nature. He has simply extirpated a long series of the most dangerous animals; other types he has imprisoned and made into house slaves. He has changed the countenance of the planet; it suffices merely to look at the earth's surface from an airplane or from the top of a mountain to see how much he changes everything. And now he is beginning with the outer world, the world beyond the earth. There can be no question of the dying out of the human species. What is more to be feared is that it will become too numerous. Now, how is something like this possible? We all know the answer: by reason. Man, although he is so weak, owns a terrible weapon, his intelligence. He is incomparably more intelligent than any other animal, even the highest. Of course, we find a certain intelligence also in apes, cats and elephants. But this is minimal compared to that which man, even the simplest, has. This explains his success on earth.

But that is only a preliminary and superficial answer. Man seems to have not only *more* intelligence than the other animals, but also intelligence of another *kind*, or however we want to say it. This becomes apparent in the fact that he, and he alone, reveals a series of very special characteristics. The most striking of these are the following five: technology, tradition, progress, the capacity for thinking quite differently than the other animals, and finally, contemplation.

First, *technology*. It consists essentially in the fact that man utilizes instruments of his own making. Some of the other animals do something similar; an ape, for example, readily uses a stick. But the deliberate production of complicated instruments by long and trying work is typically human.

Technology is, however, by far not the only peculiarity of man. It never could have been developed if man weren't simultaneously a *social being*, social in a very special sense of the word. Of course, we know of other social animals; termites and ants, for example, have a truly wonderful social organization. But man is social in another way. He grows in society through *tradition*. This tradition is not inborn, has nothing to do with his instincts – he learns it. And he can learn it because man, and man alone, possesses a highly complicated *language*. However, tradition alone would suffice to sharply distinguish man from all other animals.

Thanks to tradition, man is *progressive*. He learns more and more. And it is not a case of one single individual learning, for that happens among other animals, but rather it is *mankind*, society which learns. Man is inventive. Whereas the other animals pass along their fixed knowledge from generation to generation, each of our generations knows more, or can know more, than the preceeding one. Often great innovations come within one single generation. We have seen such an example in our own lives. What is even more striking is that this progress, so it seems, has very little to do with biological development. Biologically, we are almost indistinguishable from the ancient Greeks, but we know incomparably more.

But it seems that all this – technology, tradition and progress – is dependent on a fourth thing, namely on man's special ability to think differently than the other animals. This otherness of his thinking is not easily summed up in a short formula, for it is many-sided. Man is capable of *abstracting*, while the other animals always think in reference to the single, the concrete. Man can think in *general terms*. The greatest accomplishments of his technology can be attributed to precisely this; one need only to think of his mathematics, the most important implement of science. But abstraction is not limited only to generalities. It includes such ideal objects as numbers and values. And this is certainly tied up with the fact that man seems to have a unique independence from that law of biological utility which dominates the whole kingdom of animals. I shall introduce only two striking traits of this independence: science and religion. What an animal knows is always bound to a purpose; it sees and understands only that which is useful to it or to its kind. Its thinking is thoroughly practical. But man is different. He investigates objects, which can have absolutely no practical purpose, only for the sake of knowledge. He is capable of objective science and has, in fact, constructed such a science.

His religion is perhaps even more remarkable. We note that on the southern coast of the Mediterranean, where the vine would grow particularly well, it is cultivated only slightly because Moslems live there; just the reverse is true, under incomparably less favorable circumstances, on the Rhine or in Norway, Christian countries. When we observe the large settlements in the desert, the Buddhist and Christian places of pilgrimage, then we must admit that all of this has no economic or biological sense, that it is completely senseless from the purely animal point of view. But man can afford such things since, to a certain degree, he is independent of the biological laws of the animal world.

And this independence goes even further. Every one of us is directly aware of being free. It seems as though man, at least in some moments, could overcome all the laws of nature.

But this, in turn, involves something else. Man is capable, perhaps above all else, of *contemplation*. He is not oriented, like the rest of the animals apparently are, exclusively toward the outside world. He can think about himself, is concerned with himself, he questions the meaning of his own existence. He also seems to be the only animal that is clearly aware that he must *die*.

Reviewing all of these peculiarities of man, it is no wonder that the founder of our western philosophy, Plato, came to the conclusion that man is something different from all of nature. He, or rather that which makes him a man, the psyche, soul, the spirit, is of course *in* the world, but he doesn't *belong* to the world. He towers above all of nature.

But the above-mentioned peculiarities constitute only one side of man. We have already noticed that he is also a real and complete animal. What is even more important is that the spiritual in man is closely connected with the purely animal, with the bodily in him. The smallest disturbance in the brain suffices to paralyse the thinking of the greatest genius; a half quart of alcohol is often all that is needed to transform the most refined poet into a wild animal. Now the body, with its physiological processes and animal drives, is so different from the spirit that the question arises as to how such a connection between these two is at all possible. This is the central question of the philosophical science of man, of anthropology, as it is called.

There are various answers to this question. The oldest and simplest is the mere denial that there is anything else in man but the body and the mechanical movements of its parts. This solution is that of strict materialism. It is seldom championed today because, among other things, of the argument brought against it by the great German philosopher, Leibniz. Leibniz suggested that one imagine the brain so enlarged that one could move about in it, as in the inside of a mill. In it we would encounter only movements of various bodies but never something like a thought. Therefore, thoughts and things similar must be something totally different from simple movements of bodies. It can, of course, be asserted that thoughts and consciousness do not exist at all; but this is so obviously false that philosophers usually do not take such an assertion seriously.

Besides this extreme materialism, there is also another, more moderate one, according to which there is a consciousness but only as a function of the body – a function which differentiates itself from those of other animals only *in degree*. This doctrine is to be taken much more seriously.

It is rather closely connected to a third conception which we owe to Aristotle, and which seems to receive strong support today from science. It is different from the second kind of materialism in two points. First, it believes that it is meaningless to contrast mental functions one-sidedly with the body. Man, Aristotle taught, is a whole, and this whole has various functions: purely physical, vegetable, animal, and finally mental. They are all functions not of the *body* but of *man,* the whole. And the second big difference is that Aristotle, along with Plato, sees something special in the mental functions of man which is not present in the other animals.

Lastly, the strict platonists – and they are not lacking today – advance the opinion that, as it was formulated by a malicious opponent, man is an angel living in a machine, a pure spirit which moves a pure mechanism. The spirit, as we have said, is thought of as something completely different from everything else in the world. This doctrine, in its several variations, is held not only by the French philosopher, Descartes, but also by many present day *Existenz* philosophers. According to them, man is not a whole, but spirit alone, or, as it is often called today, existence.

As we can see, there are actually two questions involved here:

79

whether or not there is in man something essentially different from the other animals, and how this something is related to his other component parts.

But there is still another basic question concerning man which has found pointed expression, particularly in the philosophy of the last decades, that is, in the so-called *Existenz* philosophy and existentialism. We have considered the various peculiarities of man which lend him a certain dignity and power and which make him superior to other animals. But man is not just that. He is also, due to these same qualities, something incomplete, unsettled and basically miserable. A dog or a horse eats, sleeps, and is happy; it needs no more than the satisfaction of its drives. But man is different: he always creates new needs for himself and is never sated. A very strange innovation of man is money, for example, of which he never has enough. It seems as if he were essentially oriented toward an infinite progress, as if only the infinite could satisfy him.

But at the same time man, and it seems man alone, is aware of his finiteness and, above all, of his death. These two characteristics form a tension which makes man appear to be a tragic puzzle. He seems to exist for something which he can never attain. What, then, is man's meaning, the meaning of his life?

Since Plato, the greatest of our philosophers have tried to solve this puzzle. Essentially they have advanced three main solutions.

The first, which was very widespread in the nineteenth century, consists in the assertion that man's longing for the infinite can be satisfied by identifying himself with something broader, particularly with society. It is irrelevant, the philosophers say, that I must suffer, must founder, and must die; mankind, the universe will go on. We shall have more to say about this solution later on. It should only be mentioned here that most contemporary thinkers hold it to be untenable; for, instead of solving the puzzle, this solution denies the given, namely, the fact that the individual man desires the infinite *for himself*, as an individual, and not for anything else. In the gloomy light of one's own death, such theories prove to be empty and false.

The second solution, widespread today through the existentialists, maintains just the opposite: man has absolutely no meaning at all. He is a mistake of nature, a creature that has turned out wrong, a useless passion, as Sartre once wrote. The puzzle cannot be solved. We shall eternally remain a tragic question for ourselves.

There are other philosophers, however, who, following Plato, do not want to draw this conclusion. They don't believe in such complete nonsense in the world. According to them, there must be a solution to the puzzle of man.

But what could this solution consist in? Only in the belief that man can somehow reach the infinite. He cannot, however do it in this life. If, therefore, there is a solution to the human problem then man must have his meaning in the next world, beyond nature, beyond this world. But how? According to many philosophers since Plato, the immortality of the soul can be proved; others assume it without believing in a strict proof. But even immortality doesn't answer the question. It cannot be grasped how man, even in the next life, could reach the infinite. Plato once said that the final answer to this question could be given to us only by a God, by a revelation coming from the next world.

This is, however, no longer philosophy but religion. As in so many other realms, philosophical thinking here poses the question, it leads us to a borderline from which man silently looks into eternal darkness.

Being

FOLLOWING our considerations on man we should actually turn to the question of society. However, at least in my opinion, an understanding of this last problem is, to a great degree, dependent on whether or not one has clarified one's position in an entirely different realm, namely that of *ontology*, the general doctrine of that which is. For this reason, it would be more to our purpose to dedicate today's discussion not to society but to being.

This is a very peculiar realm. It is important – many contemporary philosophers hold it to be primary – but at the same time it is also very difficult. The difficulties are magnified by the fact that, at the present, we suffer under the influence of two traditions which make the access to these questions simply impossible. Contrary to the other branches of philosophy, where almost everyone at least agrees that there are questions to be discussed, ontology represents a special case: numerous older and not a few of the more recent philosophers simply deny that there is such a thing as ontology or that its problems could be meaningful. These traditions are those of positivism and of epistimological idealism. This fact implies a two-fold task for us: we must first ask whether there is an ontology, and only if we can decide for its legitimacy may we concern ourselves with its problems.

Before we ask these questions, however, it would be useful to clarify a few matters of terminology. In ontology, one often speaks of *being*, and that is being not as a verb but as a subject. It is not like saying 'it is nice being healthy', but 'being is this and that'. At least many ontologists tend to use the word in this manner. Personally, I have always found that it is better to speak not of *being* but of *that which is*. We call everything which in some way is, that is, consists or exists, *something which is*. Thus, each of my readers is something which is, and this is true also of his handkerchief or even of his good or bad mood. Indeed, the possibility that he will laugh tomorrow becomes something which is, for there *is* such a possibility; it exists, it is there. Beyond things that are, there is nothing.

As for *being*, it is the abstraction of that which is – like redness is the abstraction of red, anger the abstraction of an angry man or animal, height the abstraction of a high tower and so forth. But a fundamental rule of philosophical methods says that, when possible, all abstract words should be reduced to the concrete; for then research is easier and one is at least to a degree insured against nonsense which so often reigns in the realm of abstractions. One need only think of all the nonsense which has been written about truth, and solely because no one took the trouble to use the small and concrete word 'true' instead of the abstract 'truth'. For this reason, I shall avoid the word 'being' as much as possible and speak only of that which is.

Now, as I have said, there are opinions according to which there can be no doctrine of that which is. Such an opinion was first advanced by the proponents of epistimological idealism. They maintain that everything which can be said about that which is has already been said by the individual sciences; the only task left for philosophy is to make clear how knowledge occurs in the individual sciences, how knowledge is at all possible. Furthermore, these epistimological idealists say that being is to be reduced to thinking.

The ontologists, however, have a two-fold answer to this. First, they say that no individual science treats or can treat such questions as those for example, of possibility in general, categories, and so forth. And second, they note that the thinking (to which they want to reduce that which is) itself *is*, that is, something which is, and that the entire undertaking makes sense only in so far that one assumes two kinds of 'that which is', and then investigates their mutual relationship. But that is, say the ontologists, precisely ontology. They maintain, therefore, that epistimological idealism is basically an ontology, only a primitive and naive, because unconscious, ontology.

The other anti-ontological opinion is that of the positivists. Today, as opposed to the disappearing idealism, it is very widespread, particularly in the Anglo-Saxon countries. These philosophers maintain that when I say, for example, a dog is an animal that this is a meaningful scientific statement. But when I assert that he is a substance – substance being an ontological concept – then I'm saying absolutely nothing about reality. I am not speaking about the dog but about the *word* 'dog'. Ontology should, therefore, be replaced by a general grammar.

The ontologists, however, don't feel at all affected by these arguments. They assert that it isn't clear why one may generalize concepts up to a certain point – as the series: beast of prey, mammal, vertebrate, animal, living creature – but no further; why, they ask, this sudden leap into language? Every concrete science can be transformed into a linguistic science with the means of the present day mathematical semantics: instead of speaking about vertebrates, for example, one can talk about the use of the *word* 'vertebrate'. Once it is permitted to divide that which is into animals and plants then one may perhaps form more general divisions which no longer belong to biology but rather to a more general, in fact, the most general of all sciences and that would be ontology. These rebuttals have actually proven very influential, particularly in the United States. Some of the leading logicians, many of whom once subscribed to positivism, are today actively engaged in ontology. A classical example is Professor Quine, the well-known logician at Harvard university.

We could also formulate a third opinion. It could be asked if it is at all possible to say something general about that which is, except the trivialism that that which is, is. For it is not easy to see what other kind of statement could be made in this science.

Now, it seems to me that this question can best be answered simply by engaging in ontology, by formulating its problems and attempting to solve them. That is precisely what all of the great philosophers of the past, from Plato to Hegel, have always done. And today, following a relatively short period without ontology, we again have a great number of convinced ontologists. We shall simply follow them in some of their investigations.

But first a small question which, at first glance, seems to be very easy to solve, but which has caused much discussion during the last decades: the question concerning *nothingness*. It seems to follow from what we have said about that which is that there is nothing beyond it. And from this one could deduce that there *is* nothingness, that is, that nothingness is or exists in some manner. Perhaps this will be considered a sophism. We usually say that something *is* not or, as Sartre formulated it more sharply, there *is* nothing. An example: when the motor of a car breaks down or fails to function, someone looks in the carburetor and says 'there is nothing in the carburetor'. Now the question is: is this sentence true? Obviously it is sometimes true. But if a sentence is true then reality must be as it says it is. This is the definition of truth. Therefore, there must be nothingness in the carburetor.

Furthermore, we can *speak* meaningfully about nothingness as, for example, I am now speaking about it. But when I speak about something meaningfully, then this something must be an object, otherwise I wouldn't be able to talk about it. Nothingness, therefore, is an object. That means it *is*. And yet it is nothing, therefore it is not.

By these and similar thoughts, some contemporary thinkers – as the above mentioned leading *Existenz* philosophers – are moved to say that nothingness *exists* in some manner. Other philosophers, of course, are not in accord with this. They maintain that nothingness is only *thought of*, but that it doesn't exist at all. This question seems to me to be quite complicated and difficult. I would perhaps say the following: I would note that one must differentiate between that which is *really* and that which is *ideally*. The concept of nothingness is something which is *ideally*, and an image of a particular kind, of a deficiency of that which is *really*. That explains how we can even talk about it. Further, I would perhaps say that a deficiency can be something *real*. That, for example, my friend Peter is not in this cafe is, in spite of everything, something real. It is not merely something thought of by me but actually *is* in the cafe. Now, the question of deficiency is a very peculiar and difficult one. To me it seems clear that certain deficiencies are attached to everything we know, and this is so because all of that which is, is limited and finite. But now we are coming into very deep metaphysical questions, into the problems of the finiteness of that which is, and I would rather not touch on this here. I shall only say that, in the final analysis, that which is not is to be assumed in some way, although not in the way Sartre does it. Perhaps we shall return to this in our final discussion.

This, then, would be an example of an ontological question, and it should be clear that no individual science is in a position to solve it. Here is another question.

In colloquial speech and in the sciences one speaks of potentiality. One says, for example, that a child has the potentiality of becoming a philosopher, but a chair does not. At first, one might think that this potentiality is only something thought of by me, that there are only such things in actuality which *already* exist. But that certainly isn't the case, for the fact of the potentiality of this child's becoming a philosopher is not at all dependent on what anyone thinks about it. Even if there were no one to think about it, it still remains eternally true that the child has this potentiality.

This is, however, quite remarkable. It appears as if we should make a distinction within the real itself, that is, between *actuality* – that which is full, so to speak – and *potentiality* –

that which can become. Not all philosophers agree with this: Parmenides, the ancient Greek thinker, then the members of the Megaric school, and more recently, the German philosopher, Nicolai Hartmann, and Sartre all have asserted that the actual and the potential are basically the same. In contrast to this, Aristotle and his school believed that these must be sharply distinguished. From this arises a further ontological problem which, so it seems, has always been at the center of philosophical discussions and still is today.

This third ontological problem is that of the so-called categories. The world seems so constructed as to consist of certain things which are characterized by qualities and are connected by mutual relations. It seems as if we should distinguish three different aspects or kinds of that which is in the world, within the real. First, things or, as we, following Aristotle, are wont to call them, *substances*, like mountains, people, stones. Then *qualities*, for example, those that consist in certain things being round, others square, certain men smart, others dumb, some mountains high, others low and so forth. Finally, *relations*, as that of father to son, large to small, citizen to the state and so forth. Please note that this division has absolutely nothing to do with either actuality or potentiality, nor with the so-called levels of the actual, such as those of the material or the spiritual. All categories, so it seems, can be actual as well as potential, material as well as spiritual.

These three categories – substance, quality and relation – are, in fact, always assumed in actual thinking; as, for example, in the authoritative mathematical-logical work of Whitehead and Russell which forms the basis of modern logic. But if we stop to think about it, great difficulties arise, difficulties in respect to *each* of the three categories. Quality is something very hard to grasp; it is tempting to think of them as something unreal. A relation is perhaps even more difficult to understand since it has the peculiarity of seeming to be *between* the things in some way. Substance also offers its share of difficulties. All the things we know about an object are precisely its qualities. If we disregard them, then there seems to be absolutely nothing left.

For this reason, there has always been a philosophical conflict about the categories. Leibniz, the brilliant logician of the seventeenth century, built up a system in which there were no real relations between things. The Hegelian system, on the contrary, consists only of relations; according to it, things are only bundles of relations, and qualities are, so to speak, the expressions of relations. Still other philosophers assume, with Aristotle, all three basic categories.

This matter is of fundamental importance not only for the problem of God – different systems of categories lead to different concepts of God – but also for the philosophy of society in which, as we shall see, what is fundamental is dependent on the presupposed doctrine of categories.

In connection with this I would like to mention two further ontological problems: the problem of essence and the problem of inner relations. The first one is: is everything that is, so to speak, only a stable accumulation of qualities and relations or does it reveal a fundamental structure which constitutes it and from which additional qualities result? In other words, does man, for example, have *essential* characteristics? It seems so because it is essential to man that he possesses some reason; inessential, however, that he is, let us say, a Frenchman. Of course, everyone admits this. Numerous philosophers, however, maintain that essence itself is dependent on the subjective point of view, and is not at all founded in the real. The conflict between them and those thinkers who assume *real* essences has always been one of the most important in philosophy.

The second problem is similar and has been discussed often since Hegel. For, according to him, all the relations of a thing are *inner* relations of the thing itself in the sense that it cannot exist without them. To put it another way, a thing becomes that which it is through its relations, they constitute its essence. They are all necessary, inner relations. Other philosophers, however, believe that there are indeed some such essentially necessary relations – for example, a sense organ is constituted by its relation to the object, like hearing by the relation to sounds – but there are also inessential, nonconstitutive relations. It is inessential, these philosophers say, whether man sits or stands for he still remains a man; or, in other words, he is *primarily* man and only *secondarily* does he enter into such relations. This problem is also of great importance for numerous fields, particularly for social philosophy.

With this, we have named a few ontological questions and sketched a few examples of the problems of ontology. These are by far not all, not even all of the basic questions of this discipline. There is, for example, the very important problem of differentiating between the so-called levels of that which is, as in the series: matter, life, spirit. Is this distinction essential, as Aristotle and Hegel thought, or is it, as naive materialism and equally radical spiritualism maintain, a question only of more complex structures of one *single* basic level. Furthermore, what is the relation between existence, that by which that which is *is*, and essence, that *which* it is? What is the relationship between that which is ideally and that which is really? Should the ideal be thought of as an image of the real or, conversely, the real as an image of the ideal? What about necessity and choice in the real? Is everything so determined that it can become otherwise or is this not the case; and if not then what does the word 'can' mean in this context?

These are the questions which ontology deals with. They are difficult and very abstract questions. But whoever would infer from this that they are unimportant would be wrong. It suffices to mention Plato and Hegel, both ontologists, to realize that this science, apparently so removed from life, can be a fruitful and formative force in history and in the life of mankind.

Society

FOLLOWING these very abstract considerations about ontological problems, we return today to the question of human existence, more particularly to the question of society. I shall use the word 'society' here in the usual, everyday sense without making any distinction among the various forms it can assume, such as society in the strict sense of the word and a community. We shall be dealing, therefore, with so-called social questions.

Now, at first one might think that these are all thoroughly practical, political, economic or even strategic problems. For example, whether one should have a democracy or a dictatorship is dependent upon, one might think, which of these constitutions is more expedient. And whether private property or state's monopoly in means of production is better can only be decided by a politician or an economist, a practical man, but not a philosopher. It seems as if we are dealing here with a field that is completely alien to philosophy.

This, however, is not the case. Of course constitutions and economic structures are to be judged mainly from the standpoint of expediency, and it is also true that the philosopher has little to say about the concrete questions in this, as in other fields. For example, whether a state factory should be turned over to private ownership or not, whether the state president should be given more power or less, whether a certain state should be centralist or federalist – in each of these cases things must be judged from the standpoint of the prevailing conditions, and this is precisely what is done by the practical man, not by the philosopher.

In deciding such questions, however, it is not enough to know only the conditions. Those who say that all social matters are to be evaluated from the standpoint of their expediency thereby assert that a *purpose*, a *goal* is presupposed. Which goal? Some answer that it is not at all a philosophical question; the goal is simply the power of the state. But the philosopher asks here: why should the power of the state be our goal? Now, if the advocate of this opinion should attempt to justify his view in any way then he is no longer engaged in politics or political theory or economics but ethics, that is, philosophy. And the fact is that without philosophy, be it good or bad, scientific or dilettantic, no views at all about society can be held. For, as we said, all of these views are dependent on a *goal* and the determination of this goal is a matter for philosophy.

However, the question of the goal of social action, although central, is not the *first* question which the philosopher poses. The great, fundamental problem of social philosophy is the question of social reality. What is real in society, and to what degree? I shall only mention this question here because I believe that the solution of all other questions, as, for example, that of the dignity and freedom of man, are only a deduction from the answer which we give to the first.

Now, the situation is as follows: each of us senses that society presents itself to him as a force, a force which he can like or dislike but one which certainly can't be simply disregarded as our fantasies. For example, we are not allowed, as the great English economist John Stuart Mill once proved so impressively, to behave as we want to, even in the most liberal society. To mention just a triviality, we all must, whether we want to or not, stay within the limits of the prevailing fashion. If I were to attempt to hold a lecture in my bathing suit on a hot day – I've often had this temptation – then very embarrassing consequences would ensue. Most likely I would lose my teaching position. Perhaps I would be locked up in a hospital and my highly esteemed colleague, the psychiatrist, who is also director of this institution, would attempt, by means of the convenient injections, to improve my ideas concerning clothing on a hot day by adjusting them to fit the socially valid norms of the Swiss university world.

The fetters of society, however, are not only external. Society also penetrates into my thinking, into my feelings; it determines, at least to a high degree, my entire spiritual life. This life is, for example, considerably determined by language. But the language is completely dependent on society. Most of what I know I have learned from tradition, I have received it from society. Even what I feel and want is, in most cases, dependent mainly on my education, on that which society as a whole now feels and thinks.

Therefore, it is no wonder that society has always appeared to the thinking man, the philosopher, as a very real force. It seems to *be*, to *exist*, exactly in the same way as other real things in the world. Perhaps it is for me more of a force, even more real, so to speak, than any other component of this world.

But here we immediately run into difficulties. If we look around us, we find in society only men, I mean individual men. If, for example, I seek the meaning of the word 'mankind' then I find only individuals; mankind seems to be simply the sum of all individual men. And the same thing applies for other societies. A family is, for example, the father, the mother, children, perhaps also the grandmother and uncle, and nothing more. The German people is all of the Germans taken together. Although society presents itself to me as a real force, it is nowhere to be found, it seems not to exist in the world.

Such considerations have moved numerous philosophers – I'll call them *individualists* – to say that society is a pure fiction. In reality, only individual men exist. Together they are called 'society', but that is only a word. When one talks of the state one doesn't actually mean the state, for such a thing doesn't exist, but rather the citizens, or more precisely, those among them who exercise power. One's duty to the state, therefore, is duty to the head of the state and its officials.

Naturally you will ask me: but how can such an assertion be taken seriously? How can these individualists explain the obvious fact of the pressure which society exerts on me? The individualists, however, don't actually deny this pressure and they do know how to explain it. They claim that this pressure is the result of the mutual effect of individual men on one another. Elementary particles, let us say electrons, are also individual things but in an atom they form a whole, and this is because they mutually affect one another, attract or repel one another. The same is true for men in society. The fact that this power of attraction can be interpreted not only mechanically but also biologically or psychologically is irrelevant here. Of greatest importance is only that the sole reality in society is individual men and that the whole is composed exclusively of them.

When we reflect on this solution, however, we can find various difficulties in it. The first is that, according to this interpretation, this interaction among men must be conceived as something unreal. If the individualists assume these effects to be real then it is impossible for them to maintain that society consists exclusively of individuals. For then it would consist of them *and* all those various relationships; thus it would be *more* than the sum of individual men. An atom is also more than the sum of the elementary bodies, protons, electrons or whatever they may be called. And this argument applies even more for society.

But why aren't these relationships considered real? Solely because individualism is based on a certain doctrine of categories; for the individualists believe that there is nothing real in the world but things, substances. Everything else is said to be unreal, particularly relationships.

It might be said that these theories are foreign to life. This, however, would certainly be an error. For if individualism, as defined above, is true then it is impossible to see how society can have any rights. What doesn't *exist*, what is supposedly a mere fiction, can have no *rights*. What then results from this theory is an extreme socio-ethical individualism. Of course, only a few philosophers have risked drawing this conclusion; a laudable exception was the German thinker, Max Stirner, who wrote a book *The Individual and His Property* (Der Einzige und sein Eigentum), in which all social duties are denied. It is only to be regretted that other individualistic philosophers didn't have his courage. For it seems to me that Stirner was right; if one is an individualist, if one believes that only the individual man is real in society, then one should also be a socio-ethical individualist.

Socio-ethical individualism, however, is so obviously wrong, it clashes so completely with our insights into moral values that the whole theory must be wrong somewhere.

For this reason, there have been more than a few philosophers in history who, assuming the fact that society is something real, have built up an antithetical theory. From the ontological standpoint there are two types of such theories.

The first proposes, exactly like individualism, that only substances are real. But, contrary to individualism, it sees substance, at least full substance, not in the individual man but in society. According to it, there is only one thing, one full existant, one substance in society – the whole. Individuals are only parts of this substance and therefore not full existants. Just as a man's hand is not a full thing in itself but only a part of the whole, so is the individual only a part of society.

The other theory presupposes an antithetical doctrine of categories but draws from it a similar conclusion. It assumes that there is actually only one single category, one reality, namely, relations. Substances, like men, are then, as I pointed out in the last discussion, constituted by relations. They are what they are only by virtue of these relations; they are, so to speak, bundles of relations. But if this is so then society can and should be considered the true whole. The individual man, constituted by social relations, appears here (even more so than in the first solution) as something subordinate, something less real than society. 'The true is the whole', said Hegel, the founder of this theory. 'True' here means something like real, substantial, consisting in itself. According to Hegel and his followers, man is a 'dialectical moment' of society and nothing more.

Both of these doctrines lead to grave socio-ethical consequences, as does individualism. For if society is the only true reality, the only full existant and man only a part, an element of it, then it should be clear that man can have no individual rights. He exists *in* society, *by* society, and *for* society. This results in a socio-ethical collectivism, in fact totalitarianism according to which – although this is often denied – man essentially becomes a means and society remains the only end. Orwell, the author of the well-known novel, 1984, saw this with great clarity. During his torture, the hero asks the executioner whether the dictator, big brother, actually exists. The executioner then asks what he means by this, and the victim says: 'Does he exist in the same way as I exist?' The answer he receives is the result of social collectivism: 'You do not exist.' The individual man doesn't exist, or at least he has no full existence. He is and should always be used and ruthlessly exploited as an instrument, as a means for the whole. Such an 'element', such a 'non-being', can have no individual rights.

This is, therefore, the philosophical antinomy which forms the background for the state in which mankind finds itself today. What is real: man or society? What should be sacrificed for what? What is the end and what are the means – the whole or the individual? Are concentration camps, in which millions of men suffer endlessly and die, justified because they are useful for society, or should we say that, with respect to us, society has no rights at all; that taxes, military service, traffic laws are all morally unjustified, that we have no duties to a fiction called the state?

Common sense refuses to accept either of these extreme theses. It seems to be obvious to the ordinary man that the individual has rights of his own, but that he also must have duties toward society, that neither he nor society are fictions or 'moments'. It seems to me that we all believe this. But how can this belief, or better this insight, be philosophically explained and justified?

Such an explanation and justification is to be found, in fact, as far as theoretical foundations are concerned, as early as Aristotle. They are based, like all social doctrines, on a certain doctrine of categories. From this standpoint, not only the substances are real, real in the full sense of the word, that is, as primary realities, but also relations. Indeed, these aren't things, aren't substances, but they are, however, there; they are really attached to the substances and connect them to one another. This results in two things. First, that the only *full* reality in society are the individuals. Second, that society is more than the sum total of individual men; beside them it contains the real relations among men toward a common end.

In addition to this there is a second fundamental doctrine. The above-mentioned relations which connect us in society don't exist in a vacuum. They are founded in something, in the individual himself. This something which makes them possible is what men have in common, and dynamically, ethically seen, it is the common welfare, that aspect of the individual welfare which man not only strives for communally but also can only attain communally.

Thus, this doctrine incorporates both sides of the antimony without being one sided. The individual man, and he alone, remains the final earthly goal of all social action, of all politics. This goal, however, can only be reached by recognizing the reality of society and its own goals. But this goal is founded in the individual welfare. The duties which we have toward society are real duties; they bind us with the same moral force as those toward individuals, for society is no fiction. Yet it remains an instrument for the fulfillment of the individual's fate.

In my opinion, individualism is today no longer an important doctrine. The great debate behind the conflict of the parties and, unfortunately, the thunder of bombs, the essential debate concerning man's place in society is taking place between the doctrines of Aristotle and Hegel. It has seldom been so clear in history as it is today what a terrible, formative and destructive force the great philosophies can be. Today it is perhaps more necessary than in any other period of history for every thinking man to clarify his position in this apparently so abstract but yet so vitally important field.

The Absolute

IN THIS, our last discussion, we come to the problem of the absolute, as the philosophers are wont to call the infinite. And we come to it at the end because, for the philosopher, God, and it is with Him that we are dealing, does not stand at the beginning as He does for the faithful. If the philosopher reaches Him at all, it is only after long wandering through the realm of finite, worldly being.

A very specific difficulty of this field consists in the fact that there are two ways to God: the way of religion and the way of philosophy. Man, however, is a unity and it is not easy to separate the believer from the thinker. Thus, there is always the danger that our belief will influence our philosophical thinking, that, particularly in this question, we will assert some things as rationally proven which reason alone, philosophy, cannot establish. And precisely this is inadmissible. Whitehead once said that among the leading metaphysicians of our culture there is only one who thought about God entirely independent of belief, namely Aristotle. Everyone after him, from Plotinus on, stands under the influence of belief. Pure philosophy cannot attain more than did Aristotle. However, it seems to me that Whitehead exaggerated here. I believe that more can be said about God philosophically than Aristotle said. And from our long history we have learned *one* thing above all: the existence of God has never been seriously questioned by any of the great thinkers. That might sound strange when one thinks of the many so-called atheists. If, however, one looks at the matter a little closer then it becomes clear that the great philosophical debate isn't about the *existence* of an absolute or an infinite at all. *That* there is such a thing is maintained with the same determination by Plato, Aristotle, Plotinus, Thomas Aquinas, Descartes, Spinoza, Leibniz, Kant, Hegel, Whitehead and even, if one can compare smaller minds with greater ones, by the present day dialectical materialists, the official party philosophers of Communism. For, by denying the existence of a *Christian* God with such great vehemence, they simultaneously maintain that the world is infinite, eternal, unlimited and absolute. And what is even more, their attitude is, as anyone can easily see, typically religious in some respects. The question, therefore, is not whether a God exists but rather whether He is a person, a spirit. That might seem odd but it is so. Perhaps here and there, there are real deniers of the absolute, but, in any case, they are very rare and without any great importance. The controversial question is not, I repeat, whether God exists but how we should think of Him.

The problem of the existence of God is, of course, also legitimate. No authority, not even that of all the philosophers together, may be considered as sufficient reason for any philosophical assertion. We may and *should* ask ourselves which reasons force *us* to assume this existence.

Now philosophers, in this respect, can be divided into the two classes according to the method they use to establish the existence of God. I shall call the first intuitionists, the second illationists, although neither name is completely apt. The intuitionists believe that God, the absolute, is *directly* given in some manner. We encounter Him in our experience. It must be admitted that such philosophers are rare, or better, they rarely admit that they hold such a doctrine. This would certainly apply to the above mentioned Communist philosophers; they have never advanced a proof that there is infinite and eternal matter, thus they seem to have direct knowledge of it. The famous French philosopher, Bergson, didn't maintain that such an experience was accessible to himself or to other philosophers, but he did teach that such was true for mystics, and on this assertion built up his proof of God. These are, however, exceptions.

Among the pure intuitionists, one must distinguish the thinkers who, like Max Scheler or Karl Jaspers, assert a certain grasping of God, but who believe that man doesn't experience Him *in Himself* but in finite being. Human existence is, according to Jaspers, that which is related to itself and therein to its transcendence, to God. Thus, if it may be so expressed, he grasps the infinite not directly but indirectly, in himself, in his own being. I believe that Jaspers would protest if this were called a proof, and the same should go for Scheler, but it could perhaps be said that it is an insight into the finite being which is of such a nature as to allow a grasping of the infinite. Then the difference between this position and that of the illationists wouldn't be as great as one might at first think.

There are two kinds of illationists. Some of them – Saint Anselm, Descartes, Spinoza, Hegel and a few others – believe that the existence of God can be deduced *a priori*, without reference to the experience of finite being; from mere thinking, so to speak. The existence of God can be inferred just like the qualities of a triangle are inferred from its definition, regardless of the question whether there are triangles in the world or not.

This proof, however, was refuted by Saint Thomas and then by Kant so successfully that it is seldom championed today.

Contrary to this, numerous philosophers assume various proofs of God which are based in experience. It seems to me that most of them have basically the same foundation. I shall present it in the form which I found in Whitehead, for it seems to me that it would be generally approved by the other thinkers of this group.

Whitehead believes that we can ascertain a constant becoming in the world: everything that is, *becomes*. An apple, for example, is green and then becomes yellow. Thus, according to him, a moving force behind this becoming must be assumed. He calls it 'creativity'. This alone, however, is not enough. Given that there is something like an impulse toward the new in the world, it is still not clear why these new things should be just as they are and not otherwise. Of course, it can be said that there are certain natural laws which determine or cause an apple to become red or yellow but not blue. This, however, only postpones the question. Why are there precisely *such* natural laws among the infinite number of *possible* natural laws? Why does the world follow some patterns and not others? It can be said, of course, and it often is, that we can give no answer to this question. But Whitehead decidedly rejects this position. The philosopher, he says, is here in order to *understand rationally*, to explain. By his nature, he must assume that there are *explanations*, that reason holds sway in the world. That is the basic presupposition of science; the difference between philosophy and the individual sciences consists only in that philosophy applies rationality *without limitations*, far beyond the limits which suffice for the individual sciences. The philosopher, Whitehead says, has the right and the duty always to ask why.

One then comes to the conclusion that there *must* be a God, a force above the world which determines the course of the world, an infinite force. He calls it the principle of concretion, the reason why things are as they are and not otherwise.

Behind all of this is the following consideration which, although it wasn't formulated by Whitehead himself, is fundamental here. Why is there a world at all, and why precisely *this* world and not another? There is no reason for this to be found in the world. Only if it were the absolute would it be its own foundation. Then, however, the absolute would be given. In every instance, therefore, we are forced to assume that this is the case.

In order to avoid this conclusion there is only one possibility: one must say that there is something irrational in the world or, to put it elegantly, something absurd, senseless. Acutally all of those who deny the worth of the proof we have sketched here are irrationalists in various ways. Thus the positivists, some idealists, and finally the philosopher who has made himself famous by his atheism, Sartre. Sartre is perhaps the most intelligent and sharpest atheist whom we have ever had in history, and it will therefore be worthwhile briefly to characterize his teaching.

To a higher degree than many others, he has understood and experienced the non-necessity, the insufficiency of everything which we find in the world. All of this, he says, is without justification. It doesn't need to be but yet it *is* there. Abstract triangles, mathematical formulae are explained by something but they don't exist at all. The existence of things, this tree root, for example, cannot be explained in the same way. Real being in the world could only be explained by God. But Sartre is not willing to recognize God; he thinks He is a contradiction, and therefore he quite logically deduces that all being, particularly man, is absurd, senseless. Sartre, like no other, knows how to formulate this dilemma: one must, he says, choose between God and absurdity. He himself then chooses the absurd, the senseless. I may be permitted to remark here that anyone who knows this train of thought of Sartre cannot possibly characterize him as a mere 'existentialist'. Sartre is surely a metaphysician of the first order. Even when he errs he does it on a level many others have not even reached.

Many philosophers, however, resist accepting this senselessness in the world. Is there any sense, they ask, in philosophizing further, does any philosophical explanation still have a justification if everything that is real is nonsensical? And if such is the case, then the philosopher can and should rather assume the existence of God, in spite of the terrible difficulties that it involves, than confess with Sartre to the absurd.

Why are there these difficulties? A believer, even a believing child, knows of no difficulties in thinking with love of God. It is an intimate and clear thought, regardless of how great and sublime God may seem. The philosopher, however, is in another position. For him, God is not an object of love and respect but of thinking. The philosopher tries, must try, to understand Him.

At this point, the first and fundamental difficulty arises in the insight that God must be completely and totally different from everything else. He must be real but still have the characteristics of the ideal in a certain sense; for, by His nature, He exists necessarily like ideal being, thus also is eternal, beyond time and space, and yet individual in a certain sense of the word, even more individual than anything else, complete in Himself, 'alive' to a degree that we can't imagine. Logically, we must ascribe to Him all of the qualities which we find as the highest forms of worldly being, like spirituality, personality and so forth. But, at the same time, it is impossible to say anything about Him in such a way that our words would have the same meaning for Him as they do for all of creation. Even when we say that God *exists*, this *'exist'* must mean something else than it does for us.

And thus philosophy stumbles into a dilemma. Either we say that God is like other being, only infinitely higher in every respect, or we must assert that we can know nothing about him. But the first is obviously false. God *can't* be like other being. The second, however, is also false, for to something of which we know nothing at all we cannot attribute existence. If we have said that this something *exists*, then we have already attributed a quality to it; an empty X cannot be asserted to be, as we are taught by logic.

The best minds in the history of European philosophy have constantly struggled with this dilemma. Most great thinkers have always sought a middle way between the nonsense of anthropomorphism – that which makes God a creature – and the no less absurd nonsense of the absolute unknowability of God. An excellent example of this struggle is to be found in the third volume of Jasper's 'Philosophy'.

I am personally of the opinion that this middle road is not only possible but also exists, at least in outline form. It is the analogy solution of Saint Thomas Aquinas. I can't discuss it further here but I should like to call your attention to the fact that we today are in a position, thanks to the achievements of mathematical logic, to formulate and understand it better than ever.

That is, then, the first great difficulty. The other is in the question of the relationship of God to the world. For if He is infinite then it seems, at first glance, that there couldn't be anything beside Him, and this results in so-called monism or, if God is ascribed consciousness, in pantheism. The world would then be God or a part, a manifestation of God. Then, however, one would have to say that He, who Himself is the reason for the non-necessary, has parts, that He becomes, that He consists of finite elements and so forth. All of which are illogical.

A similar question is that of the relationship of God to the world in the dynamic order. Becoming is something which is, it *exists;* in the final analysis, therefore, it not only must be founded but also *determined* by God. In relation to the human will, this seems to mean that everything which we do or want is determined by God from the very outset and that, therefore, there is no freedom of the will.

The solution to both of these questions could be in thinking of the otherness of God and of His efficacy. God is not something else which is *beside* the things in the world and is also not, as a superficial writer once wrote, like a second horse who, along with man, pulls the boat. His being as well as His efficacy do not lie *next to*, but rather *above*, creation. It is a different being and another efficacy.

And finally, the religious question. Can the God of the philosophers – the infinite, necessary foundation of all being – be the same God as the loving father and saviour of the Christians who believe to converse with Him in prayer? The God of religion is distinguished from the metaphysician's ultimate foundation of the world in one decisive point: He is *sacred*. No one can say exactly what sacredness is, just as no one can say what color or pain is. But the sacred is given in human consciousness and in the experience of worshipping; it appears distinctly to the mind's eye. Is this sacredness identical with the infinity of the metaphysical foundation of the world? Is there any bridge at all between that which we can reach in philosophy by reason and the object of adoration and hope, the principle of love which religion proclaims?

The opinions of the philosophers are also divided on this point. No serious thinker today denies that the sacred is something primary, primary in the sense that it can be traced back to nothing else. We are dealing here with unique values and attitudes. Most thinkers today, however, believe that this realm has nothing to do with metaphysics; with respect to God there is no bridge between believing and thinking. The God of metaphysics, they say, is different from the sacred God of religion.

But there are also philosophers who don't go so far. Of course, religion says *more* about God than does philosophy.

But it doesn't follow from this, they believe, that the object of the philosophical doctrine of God should, in any point, contradict the God of religion. And such a point is actually not to be found. *Everything* that we can say about God philosophically will also be acknowledged by a religious man; its just that he knows more about Him than the greatest of metaphysicians. The disparity is not in the *object* but in the *attitude* of man. The philosopher seeks God as a rational explanation of the world. God is necessary for him, not to pray to but to preserve his rationality. His acceptance is nothing more than an uncompromising avowal of the intelligibility of being, and if one may speak of belief here, the only belief which is assumed is the belief in reason. There can be no talk of a love for God here, and when Spinoza spoke of an intellectual love of God he meant only knowledge.

This attitude, however, brings the philosopher, as in the question of man, to the borderline beyond which he sees only darkness. His God is so undefined, burdened with so many problems that the philosopher must ask himself the question – as Plato once did – whether there isn't a world beyond that of philosophy. And then he can, if he is a believer, receive from religion answers to many of his troubling questions. His concept of God will not be rejected by them, only made fuller and more vital.

Philosophy, however, can lead the thinking man to this borderline, which he couldn't cross over of his own power, only on one condition: he must remain *true to himself*. In this question, like all others, philosophy reveals itself as formative and fruitful only when it is infused with a genuine will to understand and a firm hold on reason. For philosophy is nothing more than human reason applied to an explanation of the world without compromise, without limit, and with all the dedication of which we are capable.